Teachers and Assistants Working Together

Karen Vincett, Hilary Cremin and Gary Thomas

Open University Press

Open University Press
McGraw-Hill Education
McGraw-Hill House
Shoppenhangers Road
Maidenhead, Berkshire
England SL6 2QL

email: enquiries@openup.co.uk
world wide web: www.openup.co.uk

and Two Penn Plaza, New York, NY 1012–2289
USA

First published 2005

A catalogue record of this book is available from the British Library

ISBN 0 335 216995 1 (pb)   0 335 21696 X (hb)

Library of Congress Cataloging-in-Publication Data
CIP data has been applied for

Typeset by BookEns Ltd, Royston, Herts.
Printed and bound in Poland by OzGraf S.A.
www.polskabook.pl

18-99

Teachers and Assistants
Working Together

Contents

Preface

There's a famous quotation from Henry Ford:

> Coming together is a beginning.
> Keeping together is progress.
> Working together is success.

These lines neatly sum up the issue, as we see it, for teachers and teaching assistants in classrooms. There's a need not just for understanding children's learning needs and ways of teaching, important as these are. Perhaps even more importantly, there is a need for teamwork between teachers and teaching assistants: the 'working together' of which Henry Ford spoke.

It's a serious issue. The 'coming together' has happened in the introduction of far more teaching assistants into schools in recent years: numbers have tripled over a ten-year period. But there has been less attention to the 'keeping together' and the 'working together'. It was this issue that led to the research work that this book reports.

There has been a widespread acceptance of the central role that teaching assistants play in meeting children's needs, yet few researchers have given thought to the changes that might occur when these extra people move into the domain of the teacher and how their potential contribution might be maximized. There seems to have been the assumption that teaching assistants will seamlessly slide into the classroom to work alongside the class teacher; that simply to provide 'help' for the teacher will automatically be a Good Thing. Unfortunately, the evidence shows that it isn't, and it can have effects that would not be anticipated. What is supposed to be 'assistance' can be a burden rather than a help if the people involved are not able to work as teams (see Thomas 1992).

The arrangements in which teachers and teaching assistants are finding themselves mean involvement in teamwork, but good teamwork is notoriously difficult to achieve. Evidence for the difficulty of teamwork in classrooms is provided by the history of team teaching. Team teaching began in the late 1960s with high hopes of success. It has, however, failed. Many studies, both in this country and in the USA, have shown that only a fragment of the original team teaching edifice remains. It appears that teamwork in classrooms is more difficult to accomplish than many had anticipated.

Indeed, looking at the history of teams in classrooms one could quite justifiably assert that classrooms provide an especially uncongenial environment for teamwork. One important research finding on classroom teams is that the presence of extra people in class does not automatically improve the situation for the children: having assistants in the class does not generally free the teacher for more time with the students. Rather, it can result in 'host' teachers spending more of their time *without* students. The finding is surprising yet consistent. It can perhaps be explained by the complex set of interpersonal and professional uncertainties which are introduced when extra people work alongside the class teacher.

It was these issues that led to the project on which this book is based. The Special Educational Needs and Psychology Service at Essex County Council, after discussions about its priorities for research and support to schools, recognized that support assistance was a more problematic issue than had been appreciated. Research was needed, the staff of the service realized, on ways of enabling teams of teachers and teaching assistants to work together better, and it was this realization that led to two phases of action research in Essex schools, and ultimately to a project called 'Working Together' in which teachers and assistants from Essex schools bravely agreed to experiment with different ways of working to see what effects would emerge. The results of all this are reported in the chapters that follow.

This book would not have been possible without the involvement of many colleagues, not least those in the schools in which we worked, and we should like to record our sincere thanks to them for their work, their enthusiasm and their many invaluable ideas. They include: Sharon Bradbury, learning support assistant, Sir Charles Lucas Arts College; Rosemary Cable, special educational needs coordinator, Glebe Infant School; Mandi Clarke, teaching assistant, Thundersley Infant School; Carol Connell, learning support coordinator, Colne Community School; Lucy Crowe, teaching assistant, Lyons Hall School; Glendon Franklin, special educational needs coordinator, Sir Charles Lucas Arts College; Jan Grover, special educational needs coordinator, James Hornsby High School; Paula Harris, teacher, Cressing Primary School; Philip Harverson, class teacher, Broomfield Primary School; Jackie Ketley, teaching assistant, Broomfield Primary School; Jacky Langley, teacher and special educational needs coordinator, Oaklands Infant School; Glynis Massingham, teaching assistant, Oakland Infant School; Diane McGarry, deputy head, Purford Green Infant School; Wendy Morton, teaching assistant, Glebe Infant School; Liz Nourse, teaching assistant, Lawford Mead Junior School; Collette Packman, learning support assistant, James Hornsby High School; Margaret Stone, senior learning support assistant and assistant learning support coordinator, Colne Community School; Virginia Valentine, special educational needs coordinator, Lyons Hall School; Simon Waltham, teacher, Lawford Mead Junior School; Beverley Williams, teaching assistant, Purford Green Infant School.

We would also like to thank our colleagues at the Special Educational Needs and Psychology Service (SENaPS), Learning Services, Essex County Council, the University of Leicester and the University of Leeds for their support and help. In particular, we should like to extend our sincere thanks to Erica Hempstead of Essex County Council for her efficient coordination of the meetings and the research work on which the book is based. Special thanks must also be extended to Anne Matthews, who analysed data for the first phase of the research.

Last but not least, thanks must go to Essex County Council for funding the research on which the book stands. We hope that this book will help to extend the work pioneered by Essex schools to enable innovation and experiment in teamwork between teachers and teaching assistants nationally and internationally.

Karen Vincett
Hilary Cremin
Gary Thomas

PART 1
Theory, Research and Practice on Teamwork in Classrooms

Introduction

The number of teaching assistants (TAs) in schools has mushroomed in recent years. These assistants have gone under different names (e.g. general assistant, teaching assistant, learning support assistant) in different local education authorities (LEAs), and their responsibilities have differed according to those titles. They may be employed as general classroom assistants; they may be employed to give help specifically to a child with a statement of special educational needs (SEN), or they may be employed out of the school's special needs budget to provide general assistance to teachers. The general term currently favoured by the Department for Education and Skills (DfES) for all of these staff is 'teaching assistant' and this is the term that will be used in this book, except where we are specifically referring to a specialized group of TAs such as those employed to work with children who have special needs, where we may use the term reserved for these staff – usually 'learning support assistants' (LSAs).

From 1992 to 1996 there was a 56 per cent increase in the volume of education support staff in primary schools in England, and the period 1992 to 2000 saw a 112 per cent increase. The great majority of these staff were classroom assistants (DfEE 2000; DfES 2002).

In 2004 there were 133,440 full-time equivalent TAs working in mainstream and special schools and Pupil Referral Units (PRUs) in England, this representing one full-time equivalent TA for every 3.1 teachers. The ratio in primary schools is 2.08 TAs to one teacher, as compared with nearly 5 TAs to one primary school teacher only seven years previously (DFES 2003a, 2004b).

The ratio of assistants to teachers continues to improve as policy continues to foreground the importance of assistants. Between 1999 and 2002, the government made £350 million available through LEAs to recruit an additional 20,000 full-time equivalent teaching assistants for both primary and secondary schools and to provide induction training for them.

Despite these increases and the commitment to training over the decade 1990–2000, conditions of service and arrangements for training and development have remained variable (see Inglese 1996; Loxley *et al.* 1997; Penn and McQuail 1997; Hancock *et al.* 2002). An attempt has been made to remedy the lack of coordination in training and employment practice in a range of developments, summarized in the DfES (2004a) document *School Support Staff Training and Development.* This announced plans for support staff development in which there would be developed a flexible, generic vocational qualification for all school support staff. Training would be expanded with the aim of up to 10,000 trainees progressing to a Level 2 qualification. This would be in the context of plans for the wider children's workforce with a 'Sector Skills Council' to coordinate this enterprise. The Teacher Training Agency (TTA), it announced, will take on a broader role in the education of the whole school workforce, with responsibility for defining competencies, setting standards and establishing career pathways. The document announced plans to create capacity for 7000 places for the training of higher level teaching assistants (HLTAs) in 2004–5 with an expansion of capacity to 20,000 places by 2006–7. Funding for school support staff training and development for 2004–5 would total in the region of £100 million.

These developments are made on a research base into the work of TAs that has in fact mainly been small scale. It has tended to describe at classroom level what assistants do (e.g. Thomas 1987, 1991, 1992; Clayton 1993; Moyles and Suschitzky 1997), and the work often concentrates on assistants who are employed to meet special needs (e.g. Farrell *et al.* 1999; Lacey 2001) rather than the work of TAs more generally.

The research environment and its findings are similar in the USA, where Giangreco *et al.* (2001), in a wide-ranging review of the international literature, report a top-heaviness of work reporting what is already known – on, for example, roles, lack of training or under-appreciation. Giangreco and his colleagues in particular regret a lack of research evidence on the consequences of assistants' employment on measurable outcomes in children.

Despite the lack of such research, commentary on the potential contribution of TAs is generally positive. As long ago as 1992, before the substantial increase in the numbers of TAs working in schools, Barber and Brighouse (1992) suggested an expansion and a greater involvement of TAs in teaching and learning, and the Dearing Report (DfEE 1997) recommended the development of a new qualification for teaching assistants. Ofsted (1995) claimed that there is an association between the use of TAs and the quality of teaching and learning. HMI (2002), in a wide-ranging review of TA work in schools, comment positively on the work of TAs.

The rhetoric for the benefits of additional support is therefore strong. However, surprisingly little attention has been paid to the ways in which support works in classrooms. There is widespread acceptance of the central role that TAs play in meeting children's needs, yet little research has examined the changes that might occur when these extra people move into the domain of the teacher or how their potential contribution might be maximized. Indeed, the research that does exist on the consequences of TAs' employment does not suggest unequivocal benefits.

One important finding in this respect is that the presence of extra people in class does not automatically improve the situation for the children. Indeed, a surprising finding about TAs' presence is that it does not generally free teachers for more time with students but rather results in teachers spending more time *without* them (see e.g. DeVault *et al.* 1977; McBrien and Weightman 1980; Thomas 1992). The finding can perhaps be explained by the complex set of interpersonal and professional uncertainties which are introduced when extra people work alongside the class teacher, uncertainties that are also found in situations where teachers themselves work together in the same environment (Geen, 1985).

It should be noted that one of the particular concerns about the deployment of assistants has been regarding children with statements of SEN and the best ways to provide for them. Often statements provide for the allocation of TA or LSA time to meet the needs of specific children and this has led to concerns about the 'Velcro syndrome' of child and TA becoming inseparable. Here, children may become over-dependent on adult support, or may become conspicuously identified as different. Given such circumstances, there is a need to examine the most beneficial arrangements for the working practices of LSAs who are provided to meet the needs of particular children.

In short, effective support in the classroom is more difficult to achieve than one might anticipate and it is this finding, in tandem with the large increase in numbers of TAs, that has stimulated the work that has led to this book. Everyone is certain that the expansion in numbers of TAs is of benefit, but there is less certainty about how TAs should work best to support the teacher. Who should be doing what? And how should they be doing it? This book summarizes national and international research relating to the work of TAs and gives findings from a research project organized and funded by the Essex County Council Special Educational Needs and Psychology Service to determine the effectiveness of different models for working with assistants in teams.

For the first phase of this research project, begun in 2002, we – the authors of this book – worked with six class teachers and their assistants, who had all volunteered to work with us on the project. We began by searching the academic and professional literature for information on methods of working with TAs. It transpired that there is very little such information. There are several texts that helpfully guide teachers and TAs on kinds of activity and which offer guidance on curriculum matters, but there is little or nothing on systems of organization that offers guidance on roles and responsibilities or on how *teamwork* between teachers and TAs can be developed.

We had to go back to the 1970s, to the USA and to special education to find useful research into systems for organizing the work of TAs. We located two models – *Room Management* and *Zoning* – that we felt could be adapted to help organize the work of TAs in today's mainstream schools. To these we added another method, based in team psychology – *Reflective Teamwork* – that we felt could also be used to help make the teacher-TA team more effective.

Briefly, Room Management works by ensuring that every adult in the class has a clear role to occupy. And those roles are determined by important functions that teachers, without TAs, normally have to undertake on their own: managing the large group and providing individual help. With an extra person available, the argument behind Room Management goes that these activities – difficult to fulfil simultaneously – can be separated and given to the two people. Those two people become known as the *activity manager* and the *learning manager*. The activity manager will concentrate on the larger group, while the learning manager will work exclusively with individuals, providing more intensive help in a timetabled way to a predefined list of children. The teacher of course will be in overall charge, but teacher or TA can take on either of the new roles, depending on the needs of the class and the curricular activity planned.

Zoning is a simple system that works by organizing the class into learning zones, usually structured by the placement of the groups in the class. For example, six groups may be split 5/1, 4/2 or 3/3 and these zones of groups allocated to teacher or TA, under the overall direction of the teacher. While making the allocation, thought will be given to which children will be placed where, and how the adults will be working.

Reflective Teamwork is a method of improving the planning, organization and general teamwork of teacher and TA. It does this through teamwork games and exercises and by implementing a regime of planning and reflection meetings.

We divided these methods among the teachers and TAs in the six classes and asked these staff to trial the system allocated to them. So, two tried Room Management, two tried Zoning and two tried Reflective Teamwork. We observed each class on video, examining each child in turn under baseline (i.e. before the new method was trialled) and then under each new method of organization to see how far they were engaged (i.e. doing what they were supposed to be doing). We also asked staff to keep diaries and to tell us of their experiences and feelings about the systems.

The results were fascinating. In all of the classes and with all of the systems there were significant improvements in the children's engagement. In these trials, Room Management made the most marked difference, with Zoning and Reflective Teamwork also effecting very worthwhile improvements in engagement. Despite these findings, though, staff varied in their attitudes to the programmes. One teacher who was undertaking Room

Management, for example, found the model heavy on time in planning, and difficult to mesh with the expectations of the Literacy Hour. Zoning and Reflective Teamwork were accepted much better, and some really useful ideas came forward from the staff involved for adapting and improving the systems.

It was with these new ideas and with the success of the first project that we came to the second phase. Here, we asked for volunteers from a broader range of schools, including secondary schools. Interest was high, and we worked this time with a mixture of six primary and secondary schools, but with a larger number of classes than in the first phase, since in some cases the programme was adopted across the school.

Using the detailed feedback provided by the teachers and TAs in the first phase of the project, we used an action research framework to enable participants in the programme to develop their own models from the best elements of Room Management, Zoning and Reflective Teamwork. The aim was no longer to see whether the methods were effective or which method was best – because each had been shown to have its real strengths. What we did now, in a training seminar for all staff, was to say, 'This method seems to be good for this reason and that for that reason – mix and match to develop a system that meets your needs in your circumstances.'

Our teacher and TA colleagues have gone about this task with gusto and have trialled their own adaptations, taking the best – as they see it – of these various models to fashion their own. The indications are that the new methods that they have been developing are highly effective, again enabling strong improvements in children's engagement. It also seems that the improved teamwork may be effecting improvements in children's self-esteem, and enabling TAs to feel more fully involved in the educational experience of the children.

How this book can be used

We have used our research as a cornerstone for what is offered in this book. However, we have aimed to make the book much wider than a report of research, useful as we hope the latter will be. This book will make a case for effective work with TAs which arises out of thought about teamwork, about learning needs, about openness in schools and about progressive education. It will suggest that many of the problems that have beset attempts at teamwork in the past have arisen out of confused aims and inadequate thought about the complexities of people working together. It provides a basis for effective working with assistants (as well as parents and other adults) in terms of inclusive and progressive pedagogy. It goes on to provide practical guidance on work with assistants, giving advice on management, teamwork and group organization.

We therefore hope that the book will serve a number of purposes and we are confident that it will support those who are engaged in work at a number of levels. First and foremost, we hope that it will support those who are seeking practical help in the classroom. Importantly, though, we expect that the book's theoretical and research-based elements will help those who are undertaking continuing professional development (CPD) that leads to doctoral and Masters-level research, as well as those studying as undergraduates or for foundation degrees.

With a division of the book into two clear parts, there is a clear delineation of material that is theoretical and practical. The first part examines the place and role of the TA, with a detailed look at the research that we conducted and its findings. Part 1 informs Part 2, which is wholly practical in its focus, providing guidance on making changes in organization and pedagogy where teacher-TA teams are concerned. Advice is also given in Part 2 on ways of making changes that are based in small-scale classroom research.

1 The Rise of the Teaching Assistant

As we have already noted, numbers of TAs have grown spectacularly in recent years. As Figure 1.1 shows, numbers more than doubled in the seven years between 1997 and 2004, with concomitant improvements in the ratios of TAs to teachers, as shown in Figure 1.2. It is the purpose of this chapter to examine the phenomenon of TA employment, looking at research that illuminates the characteristics of this body of people, their training, role and conditions of employment.

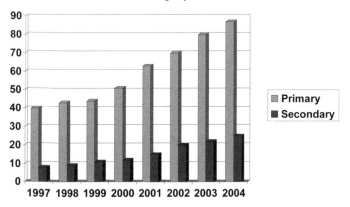

Figure 1.1. Numbers of TAs (thousands): 1997–2004

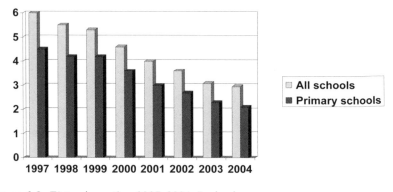

Figure 1.2. TA-teacher ratios: 1997–2004, England

Characteristics of TAs

Lee and Mawson (1998) conducted a survey commissioned by the public services union UNISON and published by the National Foundation for Educational Research (NFER). The aim of the study was to investigate the conditions of employment, training and development opportunities and the level of job satisfaction experienced by TAs. The survey was sent to 1284 primary headteachers, asking for information on TAs in their schools; 549 proformas were returned.

These schools were also sent questionnaires for the TAs to complete, to elicit their views on conditions of employment, training and job satisfaction. Surveys were completed and returned by 767 TAs.

A number of facts emerged: 99 per cent of TAs were women; 14 per cent were between 16 and 35, 48 per cent between 36 and 45, and 38 per cent over 45. Ninety-six per cent were white. Twenty-nine per cent had CSE grades 2–5, 63 per cent had O level or GCSE grade C, 17 per cent had an A level, 6 per cent a degree, 12 per cent NNEB, and 8 per cent STA (a specialist TA qualification introduced by the DfEE in 1996 – see Watkinson 1998).

Clayton (1990) collected information about the experience, training and qualifications of all TAs working in one LEA. Bringing up children, voluntary work in school, working in playgroups, childminding, work with youth or uniformed organizations and nursing were the most common types of experience that TAs brought to the job. Twenty-four had typing qualifications, 45 had qualifications from school or further education (CSE, GCSE, and degree), 6 were qualified teachers, 4 had NNEB, 8 had nursing and 18 had first aid qualifications.

More recently, Watkinson (1999) sent questionnaires to all 488 infant, junior and primary schools in Essex LEA, the aim being to collect information about the qualifications of the TAs. Similar findings to those of Lee and

Mawson, above, were made. Ninety-nine per cent were female, 3 per cent were under 25, 34 per cent between 25 and 39, 63 per cent between 40 and 49, 16 per cent between 50 and 65. Sixty-eight per cent had qualifications at NVQ Level 2 (CSE and O level), 21.4 per cent at level 3 (A level, NNEB) and 6.7 per cent at Level 4 (degree, qualified teacher, STA, SRNs). Ninety-four per cent had parenting experience, 86 per cent had experience of voluntary work and 19 per cent of childminding.

Conditions of employment

A number of research projects have investigated the conditions of employment of TAs, including contractual arrangements, number of hours worked, provision of job descriptions, appraisal and the pay levels. Two examples will be cited here, namely the UNISON research carried out by Lee and Mawson (1998) and the DfEE commissioned research conducted by Farrell *et al.* (1999).

Lee and Mawson (1998) revealed that 90 per cent of schools employ between one and seven TAs and on average schools employ four. Only 50 per cent of TAs have a permanent contract and the average number of hours worked per week is 20, half of this time being spent with students identified as having special educational needs.

Farrell *et al.* (1999) were commissioned by the DfES to obtain the views of parents, teachers, senior staff in schools and LEAs, students and TAs about the role, management and support, career structure and training opportunities for TAs. A second aim was to conduct a nationwide survey of training providers to obtain an overview of the range of training opportunities for TAs and to seek views about future developments in training.

Twenty-one site visits were made and 149 TAs, 113 teachers, 47 students and 35 parents were interviewed. Interview schedules were drawn up for TAs, headteachers, teachers, special educational needs coordinators (SENCOs), parents, LEA officers, governors and students. The research report includes condensed versions of the interview schedules. Some of the interviews were conducted as focus groups.

In most school sites TAs were observed working with students. Personal qualities such as patience, sense of humour, the ability to work as a team and an understanding of children, rather than qualifications, were found to be the main criteria for successful employment. Levels of pay were seen as too low, given the responsibilities of TAs. Contracts were too often temporary and tied to a student with a statement of special educational needs. Most TAs had job descriptions, although many staff did not refer to them and they frequently undertook work outside their remit. There was virtually no career structure for TAs and few schools had appraisal schemes for them.

Training

Smith *et al.* (1999), in a study commissioned by the TTA, discovered that 80 per cent of teachers had not received any formal training in how to manage TAs, and 63 per cent thought this would be helpful.

Fourteen per cent of TAs wished to enter teaching if a route were developed. Factors which affected decisions to undertake training included childcare, distance from home, release time from work and cost.

The qualifications most commonly provided by the trainers were the NVQ Levels 2 and 3 in childcare education and the NNEB. Half of the providers offered modular programmes; however, none offered employment-based training leading to qualified teacher status (QTS).

This project report makes a set of recommendations for the professional development and career opportunities of TAs. The suggestion is for a flexible framework for career progression, capable of responding to the diversity of prior experience and qualifications currently held by the workforce. It is acknowledged that many TAs will want to remain working as TAs – the suggestion is that they could train as specialists. TAs wishing to train as qualified teachers should have the opportunity of joining an accessible training scheme, including part-time options. This is an interesting piece of research, substantial in terms of the size and the range of methodology used.

Lee and Mawson (1998) also looked at training opportunities for TAs. Of the 767 assistants who responded, 80 per cent had access to school training days and 24 per cent attended all such days. Forty-three per cent received full pay to attend training days, while the rest were paid for only some or none of the days. In the previous three years, 74 per cent had attended a training course especially for TAs, LEA courses being the most frequent and courses in special educational needs being the most common. TAs who had worked for over 20 years were least likely to have attended a course in the previous three years and those who had been TAs for five to ten years were most likely to have attended. Reasons for not attending courses included that attendance would not improve pay, that the employer would not pay or that they had received no details of training.

The data on training were collected from TA questionnaires only. Other research (e.g. Farrell *et al.* 1999) has indicated that TAs rarely have appraisal opportunities and that training is largely ad hoc.

Farrell *et al.* (1999) discovered that the City and Guilds Certificate in learning support was the most popular accredited training course. The content of all accredited training courses was broadly similar. Three-quarters of LEAs offered training for TAs. TAs valued the opportunity to receive training, although attending training courses, either accredited or non-accredited, had no impact on salary or career progression. TAs welcomed the opportunity to be included in school training for teachers, although topics were often of little relevance. Training providers agreed with the need for a nationally recognized and accredited training programme for TAs, linked to salary and career progression, which could eventually lead to a teaching qualification for TAs who wished to become teachers. Few opportunities existed for class teachers to receive training about working effectively with TAs.

The DfES (2004a) has announced wide-ranging plans for the development of TA training during the first decade of the twenty-first century and for coordination of career development, and these are summarized in the introduction (see p. 4).

Role

The importance of TAs was first recognized by the Plowden Report (DES 1967). The Plowden committee envisaged TAs providing help of a practical, creative or sporting nature, including supervising children after school – in effect the TA was envisaged providing the teacher with an extra pair of hands.

Kolvin *et al*. (1981) described the traditional TA as a 'domestic helper'. Brennan (1982) found that the appointment of TAs in the early days of integration was mainly for children with physical or sensory handicaps – that in effect the TA was the child's eyes, ears or mobility aid. Kennedy and Duthie (1975), looking at Scottish primary schools, recommended that TAs should not plan activities, organize or manage classrooms, and their role should be restricted to encouraging students and helping them when they had difficulty.

The role of the TA has changed significantly since then and these changes are well documented in the literature. A key article is that of Clayton (1993) whose title 'From domestic helper to "assistant teacher" – the changing role of the British classroom assistant' neatly sums up these changes. TAs have evolved from doing largely ancillary work such as cleaning paint pots and mopping up spills to providing direct teaching under the guidance of the teacher.

Clayton (1993) focused on the role of the TA in Wiltshire and surveyed 72 headteachers, 81 class teachers and 100 TAs working with children with special needs in 72 primary schools. Questionnaire response rates from these three groups were extremely high at 98 per cent. Clayton found that regardless of the type of special needs, the activities which TAs engaged in were much the same. The three activities most frequently cited were carried out by 90 per cent of TAs; supervising groups engaged in activities set by the teacher, assisting individuals and offering encouragement to children. Relating students' progress to the teacher was carried out by more than 70 per cent of TAs. The data for the whole study were obtained from questionnaire surveys, interviews and documentary analysis. It is not clear from the paper which information was obtained from which source. No information is available about how the questionnaires were drawn up or how the interviews were carried out, the data recorded or analysed. It is not clear whether the different types of data were correlated and cross-checked, and it is therefore difficult to judge the quality of the research and therefore the validity of the findings.

Farrell *et al.* (1999) found a clearly understood distinction between the role of TAs and that of teachers. Teachers plan the programmes, monitor their success, hold review meetings and liaise with parents. TAs implement the programmes under the teachers' guidance. TAs tended to support students in mainstream classes by keeping in contact with those who need help, but not sitting with a student unless working on a completely different curriculum activity from the rest of the group. A wide variety of practice was observed in relation to withdrawing students from class. Parents and students understood the respective roles of TAs and teachers.

The spotlight is once again on the role of the TA in the light of the government's latest agendas to tackle teachers' workload (DfES 2002, 2004a). It is proposed that TAs will play a pivotal role in reducing demands on classteachers, including covering classes. Indeed, plans are that HLTAs will provide whole-class cover to release teachers (DfES 2003b).

The widening role is already borne out in research such as that from Eyres *et al.* (2004), which documents in a study into the perceptions of primary schoolchildren a real change in how support staff are viewed. There were changes in the perception not only of the status of the TA but also of what TAs did. As the authors put it: 'Accounts [of children] call into question the notion that teaching assistants "help" rather than teach and that there is a clear division of labour between them and teachers' (2004: 149).

Perhaps the clearest indication of the official endorsement of the widening role of the TA and the place of the TA in a team comes from a joint document produced by the DfES and the TTA (TTA 2003). This states: 'Support staff in schools make a strong contribution to pupils' learning and achievement. The National Agreement between Government, employers and school workforce unions has created the conditions in which teachers and support staff can work together even more effectively, in professional teams' (2003: 4). The same document gives useful information on standards for HLTAs (2003: 8–10).

Adult support in inclusive classrooms

Students who in the past would have attended a special school will now more than likely be allocated a TA to support them and enable them to benefit from being educated alongside their peers. This means that 'the current response to inclusion is to make sure there are extra adults available in the classroom' (Lacey 1999: 7). The role of TAs is crucial to the success of inclusive practice.

A key issue in relation to promoting inclusive TA practice is whether the TAs should concentrate only on a designated student or students with special needs or whether they should work with the whole of the class. Research shows that often the TA is allocated to work only with students with special needs (Lorenz 1998). A number of problems arise from this practice. Students can become over-dependent socially, academically and physically on adult support (Jones 1987; Lorenz 1998; Vincett 2001). Such allocation also leads to the conspicuous identification of those students as different (Jones 1987) and can prevent class teachers from getting to know students well enough to plan for their inclusion in curriculum activities. Finally, it prevents the generalized use of support being of significant benefit to the rest of the class (Jones 1987). Hrekow and Barrow conclude that 'support cannot simply be for the benefit of a variety of individual children. It must also support [classroom] teachers' (1993: 11).

French and Chopra (1999) examined parental perceptions of TAs' roles and employment conditions. Twenty-three mothers whose children received special needs support in mainstream classrooms were interviewed. TAs were seen as making useful links between parents and school staff, students and their peers, and between students and staff. Parents felt that, when TAs failed to make these connections, barriers were created between their children and the rest of the school that hindered successful inclusion. Parents believed that TAs could better make these links when they were included as team members, communicating and jointly planning strategies to enhance students' inclusion. This study emphasized the importance of TAs being allowed an equal say in discussions and planning. Parents felt that TAs deserved more respect from other school staff than they were getting, in keeping with their complex and important roles in promoting inclusion. Parents linked the status of paid adult support staff in school very closely with the status of the children being supported, equating a lack of respect for paid adult support staff with a lack of respect for their own children.

Bowers (1997) interviewed 713 students about TA support for students with SEN in their schools. Most students believed that students who received support from a TA valued that support. A consistent minority of older students aged 10 and above felt that children receiving TA support were being singled out and therefore stigmatized. Some older students interviewed also felt that TAs were not 'real' teachers. This is interesting when looked at alongside the beliefs of the parents in French and Chopra's (1999) work who felt that TAs were often seen as being marginal and not accorded much respect by classroom teachers and school management. A view of TAs as being 'lower-order professionals' or as somehow stigmatizing students by supporting them, whether justified or not, detracts from actual inclusion.

Rose collected views from ten teachers and carried out classroom observations in a mainstream school with a high proportion of students designated as having special needs and supported by TAs. Findings indicated that teachers valued the work of TAs in supporting these students and promoting inclusion and that this work was more effective through teamwork and communication. The author suggested that best practice involved 'mutual respect and confidence and a shared purpose, which can only be achieved through joint planning and evaluation' (2000: 194). The building of long-term relationships between specific TAs and teachers was also suggested as a means of promoting successful inclusion.

Giangreco *et al.* (1997) examined the support arrangements for eleven deaf-blind students aged from 4 to 20 years in the USA. All students were reported to have significant cognitive delays and additional disabilities. Data were collected in 16 classrooms in 11 public schools where students with multiple disabilities were educated in general education classrooms. The research study relied primarily on classroom observations of the students with disabilities and their teams, averaging two to three hours each, and interviews with instructional assistants, parents and classroom teachers.

Analysis of these data led to the identification of one dominant theme: the significance of the proximity between the student with disabilities and the instructional assistants, and eight distinct sub-themes, which suggested that the continuous close proximity of TAs is not beneficial for the students. It was seen to be associated with (a) interference with ownership and responsibility by general educators; (b) separation from classmates; (c) dependence on adults; (d) impact on peer interactions; (e) limitations on receiving competent instruction; (f) loss of personal control; (g) loss of gender identity; and (h) interference with instruction of other students.

Marks *et al.* (1999) looked at how paraeducators viewed their responsibilities when working with 'disabled' students (with autism, cerebral palsy, Down's syndrome and other learning difficulties) in inclusive classroom settings. All 20 paraeducators worked directly with students from Grades 1 to 8 and all had at least two years' experience. After data analysis, a presentation was made to a group of 10 paraeducators (two of them had been part of the study) which validated the following themes: many had assumed the primary responsibility for the students; they had assumed this role because they did not want the students to be a 'bother' to the teacher; they wanted to meet students' immediate needs and they had became the 'hub' or expert. This situation was generally accepted by the class teachers, who did not necessarily include the disabled students in general curriculum planning.

Lacey (1999) was commissioned by MENCAP to examine how TAs supported the inclusive learning of students with severe learning difficulties

(SLD) and profound and multiple learning difficulties (PMLD) in main-stream schools. The research was conducted in 24 schools, including primary, middle, secondary, sixth form college, all age, special schools, units, mainstream, city and rural. Schools were selected as models of typical approaches to integration and inclusion. However, there are no details included about how exactly such a selection was made. Fifty-three students (13 PMLD) and 51 lessons were observed. Thirty parents, 43 TAs, 25 teachers and 7 students were interviewed.

The study found that TAs supported students most frequently by working with groups and individuals. Many TAs tried hard not to work solely with individual students for fear of isolating them from peers. TAs adapted work and supported the responses made by students. Other duties included teaching specific targets, supporting personal and social education (including toileting and feeding), promoting safety and reminding students about appropriate behaviour. Some TAs planned and prepared work and resources, others assisted with planning, some worked from teacher plans, while others planned 'on the hoof'. Recording work, liaising with teachers, parents, professionals and reporting on progress were mentioned by all.

Participants were asked what made good inclusive practice difficult to achieve. Findings included the sometimes negative attitudes of staff to students in inclusive settings and the difficulties of finding the time for communication and planning. Other problems included teachers being unclear how to use the TA, the TA not knowing what the rest of the class was involved in or indeed the names of the other students in the class, and the TA not knowing who was responsible for their management. The amount of responsibility and work, the lack of resources and space, the lack of knowledge or expertise, the complexity of some children's disability and the poor pay were also mentioned. Only a few TAs found that teachers expected them to take complete responsibility for the students, but many felt that the teachers did not get the level of teaching right or adapt the lesson for students with SLD or PMLD.

Participants were asked what TAs needed to work effectively. Findings included opportunities to learn from observing and talking with others, training, good communication, joint planning, liaison, support and team-work, a positive approach to special needs, career structure, and adequate staff and resources.

The report concludes with pointers for good inclusive practice for TAs: working with groups not individuals; encouraging participation in lessons; care with the amount of support provided; sharing responsibility for students with the teacher; clarity over role; and time to plan with the teacher. Lacey concludes: 'TAs should not: be the child's sole minder; have sole responsibility of the child; be the child's only teacher; become a barrier between the child with SLD or PMLD and his or her peers' (1999: 24).

These studies seem to support the notion that TAs support inclusion effectively when they are valued, respected and well-integrated members of educational teams. However, TAs sometimes stigmatize the students they support and can sometimes thwart inclusion by working in relative isolation with the students they are supporting.

What effect does teacher support have on student attainment?

The last part of this review looks at the effect of paid adult support on student attainment, for all students and for specific groups of students.

Two studies looked at the effect of paid adult support on general student attainment by studying a large sample and seeking to identify differences between classrooms with and without paid adult support. Gerber *et al.* (2001) and Blatchford *et al.* (2001) deal with the issue of paid adult support as a side-issue of a larger debate about the relationship between class size and student attainment.

The Gerber *et al.* (2001) study examined data from Tennessee's Project STAR (Student Teacher Achievement Ratio). STAR was a large-scale longitudinal experimental investigation on the effects of class size and teacher aides (the American term for TAs) on academic performance. Students entering kindergarten in STAR schools in 1985 were randomly assigned to one of three experimental conditions: a small class (13–17 students); a regular class (22–26 students); or a regular class with a full-time aide. The full kindergarten sample included more than 6300 students in 79 schools across the state. Data comprised achievement scores for the students in kindergarten to third grade, and time logs and questionnaires completed by the aide in Grades 1 to 3. Background information was available for each student. Two types of analysis were performed. The first compared student achievement among the three class types with particular attention to comparisons with teacher aide classes. Analyses examined overall differences and then focused on student duration in a classroom with a teacher aide. The second set of analyses examined the duties performed by aides in the classroom and the relationship of these duties to student achievement. Complex statistical analyses were employed through hierarchical linear modelling (HLM) procedures. The results found no statistically significant differences in the outcomes for students in classes with aides in Grades K to 3 and those in classes without aides. In all cases, students in small classes outperformed those in teacher-aide classes. The study also examined the effect of length of time in aide classrooms, comparing students in aide classes for one, two, three, or four years with those in regular classes or small classes. The analyses revealed no advantage of aides when compared to full-size classes without aides. In total the analyses suggest that enduring participation in a class with a full-time aide compared to a similar size class-room without an aide may have some impact on student reading scores – at least during the grades during which reading is emphasized. The reading advantage did not continue through Year 4 regardless of how long students had attended a teacher aide class. No significant differences in mathematics performance were found in any grade.

The study also looked at the duties performed by aides and the effects of this upon student performance. Aides were asked to keep logs of how they spent their time and these were classified into administrative, instructional or non-instructional interactions with students. In summary, neither the experience level nor the educational attainment of the paraprofessionals was related to student academic achievement. The manner in which teachers deployed TAs was not related to test scores generally.

The study used large datasets from a large-scale randomized experiment and appeared to use sophisticated statistical methods to analyse the data. The authors concluded that aides do not offer the academic benefits of small classes and would not constitute an effective alternative. The performance of students in small classes was consistently superior to that of students in TA classes regardless of the number of years spent in those settings.

The Blatchford *et al.* (2001) study followed for three years a large cohort of students (7142) who entered reception classes during 1996/7 and a second separate cohort of students (4244) who entered reception classes in 1997/8. Students were followed for three years from reception to Year 2. Data were collected on class size and adult support, background details on students, student assessments in maths and literacy, teacher estimates of time allocation, teacher end of year reports on the effectiveness of classroom support and scales measuring teacher perceptions of stress, enthusiasm and satisfaction. This study found no clear effects on student attainment for additional staff in any of the three years.

There is a difference between qualitative and quantitative findings. Blatchford *et al.* (2001) investigated the perceptions of teachers about the impact of paid adult support in their classes. Their findings suggested that the use of paid adult support led to increased attention by students, effective support for students' learning, increased teacher effectiveness and increased children's learning outcomes. The authors note a marked difference between these perceptions and the quantitative evidence of outcomes.

Both these studies were concerned with the effects on average progress rather than with the impact on particular students who may be the focus of the support given. Gerber *et al.* (2001) suggested that TA support may affect specific students, affecting individual but not class test scores. Other studies support the notion that paid adult support has various effects on the learning of particular groups of students depending on the way that they work.

Roberts and Dyson (2002) evaluated a particular initiative of using support staff in an LEA. Hard evidence about the impact of the initiative on special needs in this study is lacking, given that there was no control group. However, all headteachers suggested that there had been positive outcomes for targeted students in terms of their Standard Assessment Tests (SATs) results. The TAs had planned collaboratively with the class teachers and kept records on target students' progress, which were fed back to teachers and which informed teaching programmes. Good relationships between TAs and teachers were considered by all to facilitate effective communication and efficient planning and delivery of teaching programmes. One of the outcomes of this project was a clearer role and higher expectations of TAs in terms of their potential contribution to teaching and learning. Establishing positive relationships with students was highly valued and it was felt that TAs had been particularly effective in working with challenging students. This led to benefits for the whole class in terms of the lack of disruption and improved flow of lessons.

Frelow *et al.* (1974) investigated the academic and behavioural progress made by relatively low-achieving Year 3 and 4 students when TAs were made available to teachers as part of an intervention programme. Students made significant progress in reading and mathematics, although their behaviour did not appear to be much affected, mainly because it was not an issue at the beginning.

Welch *et al.* (1995) compared two schools, one using paid adult support staff who were trained and supervised by a single resource teacher to provide supplementary drill and review to individuals or small groups of students in the back of a general education classroom. The authors of the report cautiously point towards some linkages between support and attainment/learning which is backed up by data. The maths and reading scores for some classes were significantly higher in the project school than in the control school, where baseline scores had not been significantly different. The groups in the two schools were not matched in terms of proportion of students identified as being at risk. However, these relatively tentative findings are very strongly backed up through interview and survey data with teachers and paid adult support staff.

Overall, these studies suggest that the impact of TA support on general attainment is small, but that TAs can have an effect on the learning of particular groups of students. Qualitative evidence of impact is much more positive.

An aim for the studies reported in Chapters 5, 6 and 7 of this book was therefore to evaluate the effects of different models of TA support on student attainment, given the somewhat disappointing findings concerning the employment of TAs to date. A key question to be answered concerned the *method* of working. Were there better or worse ways of working as far as the outcomes for children were concerned?

Conclusion

To date, little attention has been paid to investigating the impact on classroom practice of increased numbers of TAs. Nor has there been much work investigating the educational outcomes for students. Put simply, does the employment of large numbers of additional TAs lead to gains for the students in these classes? What is the impact, positive and negative, on teachers' practice? Given the amounts of money spent on this resource, these questions seem vital. The review of relevant research presented here shows that the limited large-scale projects on this theme take a 'broad brush' approach to the inquiry. Future research could usefully explore the detailed picture of how TAs are employed. For example, how are TAs deployed over a school day or school week? What differences are there in the ways TAs are deployed to support students with different types of need and with different severities of need? What differences are there in the ways that TAs and teachers relate to students – for example, in their use of questioning and support? Detailed case study research would complement these large-scale studies. The models being presented in this book, and our own research, will hopefully start the process of addressing these urgent practice and research needs.

2   Teacher-TA Partnership Working

While the rhetoric for the benefits of additional support is strong, few commentators have given thought to the changes which might occur when extra people move into the domain of the teacher and how their potential contribution might be maximized. Despite the fact that so much is known about effective teamwork in other areas of working life, little of this knowledge has filtered through to the classroom setting. Indeed, the practice of team teaching, which swept through schools in the 1970s, saw an early demise due to complex factors, not least of which was the teacher's need for privacy and independence. This chapter will review some of the factors that seem to be important for effective teamwork and will go on to make some recommendations for effective teacher-TA partnership working.

Johnson and Johnson (1992: 539) define a team as: 'two or more individuals who are aware of their positive interdependence as they strive to achieve mutual goals, who interact while they do so, who are aware of who is and is not a member of the team, who have specific roles or functions to perform and who have a limited life-span of membership'. Much social psychology literature is concerned with defining what distinguishes a team from a group of individuals. Katzenbach and Smith (1993), like many, stress that a team is more than the sum of its parts, and Snell and Janney (2000) define the team as 'two or more people working together toward a common goal'. In teams where there is positive interdependence, team members agree to pool their resources and to operate from a foundation of shared values. Team members' interactions are cooperative and not competitive, and a team's goals are mutually agreed rather than set by individual members.

Team effectiveness

Henkin and Wanat (1994), in a substantial review of team literature, caution that evidence of team effectiveness remains substantially anecdotal and specific to organizations, and that the findings of the few empirical studies available are inconclusive. In schools, there is minimal understanding in terms of how to make teams work (Imber and Neidt 1990). In spite of this, it is important to consider the key features of what appears to make an effective team. Teamwork literature identifies a number of themes that seem to encapsulate what determines the success or failure of teamwork.

Research findings on the effects of team size are mixed. Henkin and Wanat (1994) argue that empirical evidence for the relationship between team size and effectiveness is limited. For example, Gladstein (1984) showed a negative relationship between increasing team size and effectiveness, while Magjuka and Baldwin (1991) found no relationship. Buchanan and Huczynski (1985) suggested that the ideal team size is no more than 12, West-Burnham (1991) that the best teams have a membership in single figures, and Handy (1993) that the number is as small as 5 to 7. Virtually all effective teams found by Katzenbach and Smith (1993) ranged between 2 and 25 people. West (2000) has shown that any team needs a rich diversity of input to be creative and that the best size for a high functioning work team is around 7. As teams get larger, satisfaction and ease in talking diminish proportionately (Buchanan and Huczynski 1985). Large groups also experience difficulty in agreeing on specific actionable tasks (Katzenbach and Smith 1993). In reality, for the classroom teams that are the focus for this book, the size of the team is relatively small.

There is a considerable body of literature which stresses the importance of teams being clear as to their purpose (Galagan 1986; Shea and Guzzo 1987). Despite this, Senge (1990) argues that teams are frequently set up without any clearly articulated function. Handy (1995) notes the importance of clarity over the task to be undertaken, including timescales, importance of the task and required standards. Skill variety, task significance, autonomy and responsibility for outcomes are important for effective performance (Hackman 1987). Hardaker and Ward (1987) demonstrate that a clear understanding of mission among process quality management teams is crucial for their success. In schools, Georgiades and Keefe (1992) demonstrate that the mission, goals and expectations must be set and clearly communicated. Teamwork in an educational setting might entail tasks such as setting goals, identifying problems, assessing students' needs and skills, exchanging information, brainstorming, problem-solving, and making implementing and evaluating plans. Johnson and Johnson (2000) argue for the importance of group goals as opposed to individual goals. They cite Matsui *et al.* (1987) and Mitchell and Silver (1990) whose work indicates that group goals, compared with individual goals, result in higher group performance, greater goal acceptance and more cooperation among group members. In relation to teacher-TA teams it is often the case that these teams do not have opportunities to reflect on their purposes and goals.

The concept of role has been seen as fundamental to the understanding of social systems (Kahn *et al.* 1964). Given the findings of the research mentioned above (e.g. Farrell *et al.* 1999; HMI 2002) relating to the lack of clarity around TA roles, this would appear to be an important area for consideration in developing teacher-TA teams. Looking at roles in education, Hargreaves (1972) identifies six basic varieties of role conflict, all arising from different sets of expectations. Stress may arise because roles are not well defined or because an individual is unsure about appropriate behaviour. Firth (1983), in reviewing case studies from her own experience as an occupational psychologist, suggests that stress at work is caused by ambiguity, inadequate feedback and uncertainty in relationships.

Johnson and Johnson (1992) discuss personal responsibility in achieving team goals. Team members reduce their contributions to goal achievement if they cannot identify with those goals, or do not feel accountable. If there is high individual accountability, if it is clear how much effort each member is contributing, if redundant efforts are avoided, if every member is responsible for the final outcome and if the group is cohesive, then individuals are likely to be more hard-working (Messick and Brewer 1983). Drucker (1994) suggests that team success depends on matching people to task, based on a clear understanding of the requirements of each task and the abilities of each person. In classrooms, such matching is often missing – with no analysis of the task to be done, or the best person to do it (see Thomas 1992).

Teams also need to have the appropriate mix of skills necessary to undertake the job. These requirements fall into three categories: technical or functional expertise, problem-solving and decision-making skills, and interpersonal skills (Katzenbach and Smith 1993). Effective teams require members with the skills and knowledge needed to address problems systematically (Mohrman and Ledford 1985). Teams can, however, acquire the requisite characteristics through training (Sundstrom *et al.* 1990).

Handy (1993) looked at the skills and abilities of team members and how these relate to the team's tasks. He found that people who are similar in their attitudes, values and beliefs tend to form stable, enduring groups, since homogeneity tends in general to promote satisfaction. Some research, however, indicates that heterogeneous rather than homogeneous groups are more likely to be creative and to reach high-quality decisions (Hoffman 1979; Johnson and Johnson 1992). This applies particularly when working on complex, non-routine problems that require some degree of creativity – such as those faced in classrooms on a daily basis. Disadvantages of homogeneous groups are that they lack the controversy and conflict which has been shown to be essential for creative thinking. They also tend to be risk avoidant (Bantel and Jackson 1989) and they more frequently engage in 'group-think' (Janis 1983). Thomas (1992) found that heterogeneous class teams of teachers, support teachers and TAs working together in primary and secondary schools had fewer difficulties than homogeneous teams.

Much of the research into effective teams suggests that members' learning styles affect the functioning of a team. Honey and Mumford (1986) defined four different learning styles: activist, reflector, theorist and pragmatist. They suggest that within any team all learning styles should be present since teams need to be able to accumulate knowledge from different sources at different times. Wallen (1963) noted that all groups need membership roles which include a logical thinker, a strong fighter and a friend and helper if they are to function effectively. Building on this work, Belbin (1981, 1993) completed studies that analysed the functions present in the most high-performing business teams. He identified eight roles that are needed for a fully effective group. He called them the chairman, the shaper, the plant, the monitor-evaluator, the resource-investigator, the company worker, the team worker and the finisher. Individuals can take on more than one role or the characteristics of more than one can be amalgamated. In relation to teacher-TA teams, it would seem that diversity in skills, abilities, teaching and learning styles, and knowledge is to be welcomed in order to provide the best possible learning environment for students.

There is considerable research looking at the contribution of teambuilding to effective teamwork. Several teambuilding courses have been shown to have positive outcomes. These can be summarized as: more positive attitudes and job satisfaction (Barker 1980; Kersell 1990; Lowe 1991); greater understanding and communication between team members (Barker 1980; Whalley 1992; Rainbird 1994); development of new skills (Barker 1980; Kersell 1990; Lowe 1991); and higher productivity or new designs (Lowe 1991; Crom and France 1996). Shonk (1992) suggests that teams should use teambuilding events to explore together what is most appropriate for them in terms of how they should meet, communicate and make decisions.

Despite these findings – findings that essentially reinforce good common sense – Rottier (1996) notes that most teachers in the USA have little or no staff development in how to function in a team, and suggests this should form part of staff development activities. Farrell *et al.* (1999) found a similar picture in British primary schools, with most classteachers having no training in how to work effectively with a TA.

In the literature on multidisciplinary teamwork, there is clear evidence of the benefits of training people from different disciplines together (Horst *et al.* 1995; Carpenter and Hewstone 1996), although difficulties in designing and implementing joint training courses have been identified (Wood 1994). There are some studies which demonstrate the benefits of shared learning opportunities (Horst *et al.* 1995; Carpenter and Hewstone 1996), in particular improved understanding between professionals. Joint training, where the teacher and TA attend courses together, is increasingly popular. The DfES induction training courses are an example of this. In Essex LEA, TAs and teachers are encouraged to attend courses in pairs (e.g. on autism and Down syndrome) as part of the inclusion strategy. Actively training to build effective teams, however, is still rare.

Communication has been identified as a vital ingredient of effective teamwork and this has attracted considerable interest from researchers. Rainforth *et al.* (1992) suggest that interaction is particularly important when teams are first set up. Katzenbach and Smith (1993) found that successful teams gave themselves time to learn to be a team, and that the first meeting is particularly important in setting the tone for future meetings. Much of the literature on effective communication focuses on the importance of clarity (Johnson and Johnson 2000) and active listening (Lacey 2001). Johnson and Johnson stress the need for 'frequent and regular meetings that provide opportunities for team members to interact face to face and promote each other's success' (2000: 553). There are many techniques available in the literature that can aid a team in working through problems together. Henkin and Wanat (1994), for example, describe a school which set up a number of teams to look at the problems of low reading scores in schools. The teams were given training in methods including force field analysis, nominal group technique and proposal weight analysis. Conversely, defensive behaviour in a group can occur when people feel misunderstood or threatened. Gibb (1961), in an eight-year study of communication, demonstrated that defensive behaviour is correlated with losses in efficiency and effectiveness. Messages that led to defensiveness included those that suggested a member was evaluating or judging other group members, or was trying to control them. Communications that reduced defensiveness included messages showing empathy and respect for the receiver.

Sundstrom *et al.* (1990) found that physical environments that facilitate informal, face-to-face interactions enable strong inter-member communication patterns and higher levels of group cohesion. Bredson (1989) argues that in schools it is essential to break down the traditional isolation in the classroom. Henkin and Wanat (1994) suggest the importance of team members working in open environments with frequent opportunities for interaction. Clearly, TAs and teachers need time to meet and plan together (Linder 1990; Losen and Losen 1994), but prioritizing the time for this is often seen as problematic (Farrell *et al.* 1999).

Leigh (1996) and Rottier (1996) argue for the commitment of senior management to teamwork, including articulating a clear vision of what a successful team looks like and monitoring team effectiveness. Rottier suggests that if the organization is genuinely committed to teamwork, then recruitment and selection procedures should focus on the candidates' ability to function in a team. There is also evidence that teams function more effectively if they are provided with regular feedback about how well they are doing (Garvin 1988). Information access, the extent to which managers and supervisors provide information and data to team members, appears to be significantly related to team effectiveness (Magjuka and Baldwin 1991). Linked to support from the management is a supportive organizational culture. Organizational culture refers to the collective values and norms in an organization. Shea and Guzzo (1987) suggest that values such as shared expectations of success may foster team effectiveness. Organizational values like attention to detail, discipline and continuous improvement tend to pervade an entire organization and its teams (Henkin and Wanat 1994). There are examples in the literature which appear to confirm that the presence of a supportive organizational culture is positively associated with the effectiveness of teams (Peters and Waterman 1982; Galagan 1986).

Empowerment and autonomy of teams appear to be important determinants of effectiveness. Morgan and Murgatroyd (1994) describe the concept of total quality management (TQM) with its belief that quality is the responsibility of the whole workforce. Kawahito and Kiyoshi (1990) attribute 'quality circles' to the success of labour relations in the Japanese automobile and steel industries. A quality control circle has been defined as a small group of people who do similar kinds of work and meet to identify and solve product quality problems. Quality circles annually produce thousands of specific improvements in product quality, safety, cost reduction, communication and efficiency. Japanese participants in quality circles not only identify the problem at their workplace but also find and implement the best solution by themselves.

There have been many studies looking at the effects of power in teams. Johnson and Johnson (2000) found that the effectiveness of groups improves when power is relatively balanced among the members, and when power is based on competence, expertise and information. The ability of groups to solve problems increases as all team members come to believe that they influence the direction of group effort equally, and as the group climate becomes relatively free of domination by a few. When members have equal power they are more cooperative in their interactions, and more committed to implementing the group decision. Studies have found that the satisfaction of subordinates within an organization increases when they believe they can influence particular aspects of the organization's decision-making (Tjosvold 1991). Unequal power interferes with the trust and communication necessary for managing group conflicts constructively.

Johnson and Johnson (2000) have also shown that communication is affected by the status of members. High-authority members do most of the talking, while low-authority members do not communicate very much with each other during a group meeting, preferring to address their remarks to high-authority members. Johnson and Johnson (2000) suggest actively pursuing equal participation of all members and the valuing of all members' ideas and views, regardless of status. This issue is highly relevant to teacher-TA teams, where differences in status come into play. Research investigating

TAs in British primary schools suggests that they are concerned about their lack of status, pay, contract, training and role clarity (Clayton 1990; Lee and Mawson 1998; Farrell *et al.* 1999; Watkinson 1999). The Centre for Studies on Inclusive Education (CSIE) suggest that the 'white coat' image of special needs disappears if teachers and TAs value common-sense solutions to everyday problems (CSIE 1995: 5). If teachers and TAs assume that certain educational needs are only soluble in the presence of specially trained experts, then movement to inclusion will be slow.

Some have argued that effective teamwork and creative problem-solving in schools has been compromised in recent years by a lack of teacher autonomy. New Labour's continuation and extension of Tory education policy has been coined 'new managerialism' by a number of commentators (e.g. Ball 1997; Randle and Brady 1997; Welch 1998; Gewirtz and Ball 2000). Parker-Rees (1999) notes that 'we have become too accustomed to the assumption that educational practice must be tightly controlled by policy and that management must determine, from above, what teachers should deliver and how they should deliver it' (1999: 2). Woods (1995) has shown that it is possible for teams within schools to develop creative and inspiring approaches to teaching, although they often pay a high price for holding out against the prevailing culture of new managerialism. The report *All Our Futures: Creativity, Culture and Education* (NACCCE 1999) found that 'many schools are doing exciting and demanding work, but often see themselves doing this despite, not because, of the existing climate' (p. 8). The very concept of teachers and TAs engaging in teamwork and creative problem-solving could therefore be described as 'counter-cultural' within the current educational climate. This will need to be borne in mind as teacher-TA teams use 'a conversational approach' (Parker-Rees 1999: 7) to increase communication, planning and teamwork, and to strengthen relationships and communities.

Team teaching

The difficulties encountered by the emergence of teacher-TA teams echo many of the problems described in research into team teaching. In the early 1960s, team teaching (meaning teaching by groups of qualified teachers working together) was heralded as a new and innovative method which would bring rich rewards. Geen (1985) traced the history of team teaching in England and Wales and identified reasons for schools abandoning it because of the time and energy consumed by planning, the reluctance of some teachers to teach in front of colleagues and differences in ideologies between team members. Similar results were found in the USA. Cohen (1976) suggested that the decline in team teaching was due to the amount of coordination and communication needed for effective functioning of the larger group.

Associated with successful team teaching were attention to team dynamics and the support of the school management. Hatton (1985) reviewed research into team teaching in the UK, USA and Australia and concluded that teacher culture strongly supported an individual orientation to teaching. She found that teachers tried to maintain privacy, and felt embarrassment and intimidation when others were present. Teachers would arrange 'alternative cover' for themselves when the barriers afforded by classroom walls were removed – for example, in open-plan classrooms by re-arranging the furniture. Many writers have drawn attention to the difficulties of two teachers working together (e.g. Fish 1985; Jordan 1994). Thomas (1992) demonstrated that the mere presence of someone else in the room led to personal and interpersonal tensions and differences of opinion. Other problems included agreeing on the task, finding time to plan and mismatches in ideology. Thomas suggests that collaboration is not a natural thing for teachers to do in the classroom. Research into the views of classteachers suggests that they find that they are not trained in the management and deployment of TAs and that they have insufficient time for planning and for meeting with the TAs who work in their classes (Farrell *et al.* 1999). In addition, they are unsure of how best to use TAs and find some TAs lacking in the knowledge and skills needed (Lee and Mawson 1998; Smith *et al.* 1999). Inglese examined the reciprocal perceptions of supporters and teachers concerning the role of the other. Very few of the classteachers questioned had had any training for working with support staff, almost all of them regarded the support staff as possessed of special non-transferable skills (which did not, however, include much knowledge of curriculum requirements) and 'many found advisory suggestions difficult to incorporate in the classroom' (1996: 85).

Research in the USA on effective schools suggests that 'team configurations are the single most effective way to deal with problems currently facing public schools' (Scarp 1982: 50) and that the participation of teachers in groups is associated with positive changes in individual attitudes and enhanced organizational effectiveness (Conley *et al.* 1988). These findings, however, are not borne out in other major studies. De Vault *et al.* (1977) noted that having volunteers and aides in the class did not generally free the teacher for more time with students, but rather resulted in the teacher spending more time without students – on administrative and non-teaching activities. Strain and Kerr's (1981) review of the major findings on the educational effects of mainstreaming in the USA provides evidence that improving adult-child ratios does not in itself have beneficial effects for children with SEN. In special classes, where assistance was available to the teacher on a far more frequent basis than in mainstream classes, children with special needs did not achieve significantly better educationally than matched groups of children in regular classes. In mainstream classes where additional help was provided, benefits could not be shown for children with special needs unless special arrangements were made for the working arrangements of the additional personnel. Clift *et al.* (1980), in their study of 40 nurseries, looked at the nature of adults' activities. Teachers spent most of their time on children's activities and administration; assistants spent more time on housework (routine activities) and equipment. This research found that a plateau occurs in the benefits accorded by having extra adults in the classroom: most involvement with children occurred when three adults were present – beyond this there was no improvement.

There is another dimension to teamwork, problem-solving and support which should not be understated, and this is the support which is given by peers, parents and community volunteers. Tizard and his colleagues demonstrated some time ago (1982) how parental involvement in helping children to read can produce remarkable improvements in reading ability. Their 'low-tech' approach is consonant with the spirit of inclusion for two reasons. First, specialist assessment and curricular 'treatment' are played down while the value and legitimacy of simple pedagogy is reinforced. Second, the contribution of the parent (and other volunteers) is given credence. Tizard's findings killed the assumption that there is a special set of pedagogic skills accessible only to those highly qualified in education. Even more important, Tizard laid to rest the idea that children who were experiencing difficulties at school needed an extra-special set of pedagogical skills and methods to help them.

It is not only parents who can provide extra support, but also peers. Any attempt to equalize power in the classroom through the development of effective teams must take account of the children who are an intrinsic part of classroom teams. Leyden (1996) stresses that all children, even those with significant special needs, can benefit from peer and collaborative learning experiences and suggests that adult and peer support is complementary. He reviews evidence which demonstrates the wide range of benefits – curricular and social – which can come from peer tutoring and other forms of peer support and collaborative learning. These successes arise not only when the tutor is the mainstream student, but also when it is a 'learning disabled tutor' (1996: 52). Pugach and Johnson (1990) give helpful advice on how the teacher can share expertise with peers and parents, separating the strategic thinking and planning from the 'doing'.

Conclusion

In summary, there is a great need for effective teamwork in classrooms if we are to avoid creating cultures of dependency among students, and poor communication and ineffective working among staff. Teamwork is more difficult to achieve than one might anticipate, and it is this finding in tandem with the large increases in the number of TAs that have stimulated the work which has led to this book. Much is known about how teams work effectively and productively in other areas of working life, but little of this has been applied to a school context. The next chapter gives our first response to this emerging need for the principles and practices of effective teamwork to be applied to educational settings. Before this, though, key principles for developing effective teacher-TA teamwork are distilled in Box 2.1 from the literature reviewed in this chapter.

Box 2.1. Key principles for effective teacher-TA teamwork

 1 Senior managers demonstrate commitment to teamwork, which might include a vision for successful classroom teamwork, non-contact time, venues for training and meetings, and review and feedback on performance.
 2 Classroom teams are clear that they are a team and value positive interdependence.
 3 There is a recognition that teamworking skills can be learned. Teambuilding training and ongoing support might include areas such as effective communication, problem-solving and dealing with controversy.
 4 Team members have a strong role in defining effective practice for their classroom teams.
 5 Teachers and TAs have opportunities to reflect on, share and agree their common aims, goals and roles within the team.
 6 The team knows what it is expected to deliver. Both the teacher and TA are committed to this.
 7 Goals relate to work undertaken in the classroom and also to team processes.
 8 TAs are allocated to work with a limited number of teachers so that they can spend time getting to know them.
 9 Classroom teams have good communication systems. TAs and teachers have time to plan and evaluate together.
10 Meetings are carefully structured, with clear roles and opportunities for all to give views, regardless of status.
11 Time for teachers and TAs to meet outside of teaching time is accounted for in pay structures and cover costs.
12 Teachers and TAs participate in at least some joint training.
13 Teams feel empowered and use their autonomy effectively to solve problems.
14 Classroom teams self-evaluate regularly against joint and individual performance targets.
15 Teams frequently celebrate.

---

3 Meeting Children's Needs – Reflective Practice, Reflective Teamwork

Defining the job of the teacher isn't easy. Teachers are educators, administrators, managers, surrogate parents, liaison officers, social workers and much more.

If teachers' jobs are so diverse, what do TAs do? Do they take over some of a teacher's roles, leaving the teacher to concentrate on core teaching tasks? Or do they do a little of everything that the teacher does – always, of course, under the teacher's direction?

Twenty years ago, the answer would almost certainly have been that the TA (probably then called an auxiliary or ancillary helper) had a limited range of tasks to fulfil, and that this range of tasks excluded teaching. Sometimes this led to TAs being thought of simply as 'bottle-washers and bum-wipers'.

Today the picture is very different, as we indicated in Chapter 1. Today, TAs are thought of as assistants who teach, and not merely as assistants to the teacher. This move to more responsibility is of course controversial, especially as pay for assistants is so low relative to that of teachers. When more is asked of TAs, questions of exploitation arise, as well as questions about whether TAs can be expected to undertake work for which they have not been trained.

It is our experience, though, that most assistants welcome the opportunity to become involved in a broad range of classroom activity, and find great reward in helping to foster children's cognitive and social development. In many ways, it is artificial to try to separate out the many different things that happen in a classroom and to say that this group of activities is concerned with administration or housekeeping or display, while that group is concerned with cognitive growth or social development. We firmly believe that everything that happens in a classroom – every interaction, every conversation – is an opportunity for children to learn in one way or another. And we equally firmly believe that TAs, most of whom have a wealth of experience, are able to foster that learning.

It is these beliefs that encourage us to suggest that TAs can and should be involved in the broadest range of activity in the classroom, and much of this book is based on the supposition that TAs nowadays fulfil a wide range of tasks that parallel or shadow those of the teacher. In fact, the organizational advice given in Part 2 of this book is given on the assumption that the teacher and the TA can each adopt roles that are pedagogic, administrative or even in some ways managerial. When this organizational focus takes centre stage, questions about whether TAs should concentrate only on a 'designated' child, or if they should work with the rest of the class, become less relevant.

We believe therefore that the employment of TAs and teachers is at an important stage currently, when these organizational issues come to supersede those narrower questions about specific role.

Before moving on to those organizational considerations in subsequent chapters, we explore in this chapter some facets of the classroom that are about children's learning and growth. There is now a wealth of evidence about the role of the TA in respect of fostering children's development and some of that is given here. It is our feeling, though, that in providing evidence of other people's successes we should not be aiming to provide blueprints for action elsewhere. We believe that experiences – of success or failure – are best thought of as food for thought, providing stimulus for reflection and development.

It is in this spirit of questioning and reflection that this chapter is provided. There are therefore no apologies if there seem to be more questions here than answers.

Questions are vital for reflective practice. *Reflective practice* is a term that is often heard in relation to the work that teachers do, and it is as relevant for TAs as for teachers. It essentially means nothing more complicated than thinking about what you are doing. It means deliberately posing yourself questions, experimenting with solutions, learning from experience and using that experience to adjust how you respond to a similar situation in the future. It means having ideas, planning, reviewing how plans worked out, and revising. It means thinking, and being prepared to change what you do and how you behave. All of this is in the context of reading, listening to others and learning from research where it appears to be relevant to your own practice. Donald Schön, a well-known exponent of reflective practice, or *reflection in action*, puts it thus:

> It involves a surprise, a response to surprise by thought turning back on itself, thinking what we're doing as we do it, setting the problem of the situation anew, conducting an action experiment on the spot by which we seek to solve the new problems we've set, an experiment in which we test both our new way of seeing the situation, and also try to change that situation for the better. And reflection-in-action need not be an intellectual or verbalized activity. If you think about – my favourite example of reflection-in-action

is jazz, because if you think about people playing jazz within a framework of beat and rhythm and melody that is understood, one person plays and another person responds, and responds on the spot to the way he hears the tune, making it different to correspond to the difference he hears, improvization in that sense is a form of reflection-in-action.

(Schön 1987: 1)

Open-mindedness, flexibility and a willingness to listen and change are the key elements of reflective practice and it is interesting that these features also characterize good teamwork. One could perhaps talk about the *reflective team*, a team that considers not just how it works together as a unit but which, as part of this process, also collectively thinks about aspects of learning and pedagogy. We go on later in this book to describe *Reflective Teamwork*, a way of facilitating the team's coherence and effectiveness, but we make in the present chapter some suggestions for structuring thought about pedagogy and learning in order to help frame that teamwork.

What kind of help?

In the rest of this chapter we try to make it clear that we believe that learning is continuous and that every situation has to be assessed for what can be gained from it. However, it is nevertheless worth stating at the outset a few broad features that are understood about learning and that it is useful to consider in the classroom. These are given in Table 3.1.

Table 3.1. How learning takes place best

Learning takes place best ...	*Things to consider*
... in a stress free situation. None of us can learn well when we are under pressure, and children are no exception.	Is the student being pressurized to learn? How can advice or correction be offered without disapproval or irritation?
... when the activity is at the right level – not too hard and not too easy. The psychologist Vygotsky (1978) talked of a 'zone of proximal development' (ZPD), by which he meant that children learn best when they are doing activities that they	How can you find out what is in the child's ZPD? What could you do to check whether the work is too easy or too hard?

cont.

Learning takes place best ...	*Things to consider*
are just on the borderline of undertaking independently. They should not struggle, but neither should they 'sail through it'.	
... in regular, small doses. For example, four sessions each of 5 minutes are better than one of 20 minutes.	How can learning be divided in this way?
... when students are getting plenty of help. One doesn't need to be trained or expert to help. One needs merely to be more skilled than the learner. The relationship is of mentor and apprentice.	Always help students if they look as if they need it. To have long periods waiting for a child to respond merely promotes feelings of failure.
... when it is fun. Learning is fun if it is in a natural context – if the learner can see a point to it. If this is the case, learning is always a pleasurable experience.	Try to make all learning situations relate to the child's own experience in some way.
... when it is rewarding. If the task in itself can be rewarding, this is ideal. Sometimes children may need additional rewards – for example, praise from their mentors.	If the activity itself makes sense to the child it will be reward in itself, but remember also to praise a child for success. Your own affirmation of children in their activity will be very important to them.

For all children, but particularly for those who are being included, it is worth asking a series of questions about what is being done in a teaching session, and how it might be changed. Udvari-Solner and Thousand (1995) suggest thinking about the following:

- the format of the lesson;
- arrangement of groups;
- changes in approach to teaching;
- adapting the goals being set for children (sometimes called 'differentiation by outcome');

- use of materials and how these might be changed;
- amount of personal support (more or, possibly, less);
- adapting the task (sometimes called 'differentiation by activity').

Alongside such an *aide-mémoire*, it is, as we noted at the beginning of this chapter, important to be reflective – to think about what is happening and to use one's personal experience and judgement for guidance. We therefore give here a couple of reflections about learning in the classroom, both for the direct impact of the material being related, and as examples of the process of reflection.

The first one is taken from a piece by Tony Booth and draws from observations he made in a primary school. It points to the real-life situations in which TAs find themselves – sometimes in roles they know are best avoided. For example, they may find themselves acting as the child's servant, rushing up to help at the first sign of difficulty; or as a kind of workplace supervisor, pushing children to meet the teacher's production targets. Booth describes how the combination of these roles can be detrimental to the child's full involvement in an inclusive classroom:

> I observed Carol, who has Down's syndrome, in several lessons. Because of the level of support she received 'she' always completed the work, though some activities had little meaning for her. However, I only saw her as a full participant in a classroom, caught up in the general chat, when she was supported by a special needs assistant who claimed to have hated school and joined in the general flow of fun and mild disruption herself.
>
> (Booth 1996: 96)

The second is taken from Swann (1988), who encourages all who work in classrooms to think about the learning that happens there. The question he is posing is whether learning is confined to the formal parcels of time into which it is officially supposed to be packaged at school, for example that which happens under the aegis of the National Curriculum. For Swann, it is emphatically the case that the National Curriculum does not circumscribe all that is learned in the classroom. Talking of special needs (although his analysis could apply to any classroom situation), Swann draws attention to the absurd notion of 'access to the curriculum' and suggests that what this phrase implies is teachers 'prising open the doors of a department store for the benefit of the masses. "The curriculum" is there for the taking, if the key can be found' to enable the access (1988: 98). As Swann makes clear, the curriculum is more usefully seen 'not as knowledge to be conveyed but as a set of teaching and learning relationships by which that knowledge is conveyed' (1988: 98).

Swann's insightful analysis reminds readers that the concerns of school staff, often encouraged by the strictures of the Office for Standards in Education (Ofsted) to meet the demands of the National Curriculum, should not be a straitjacket that constricts spontaneity, creativity or imagination in classroom activity. It should not inhibit us from encouraging students' development whenever the opportunity arises. In a case study of a profoundly and multiply disabled girl in a vibrant primary classroom, Swann shows how the girl is included by being accepted on the basis that she is able to learn at her own pace. Her inclusion came only because she had been *exempted* from the National Curriculum and from normal expectations.

Children's learning does not come about through the formulaic use of techniques or procedures, nor through fundamentalist adherence to the edicts of the National Curriculum. Rather, it lies in providing opportunities for learning and sensitively fostering that learning wherever possible.

What kind of promotion of social activity?

Learning how to live with others is one of the most important facets of learning that occurs at school and opportunities for natural, unstructured interaction should of course be maximized. Salisbury *et al.* (1995) investigated the strategies used by teachers (as distinct from specialists) to promote social inclusion in classrooms. These included:

- the setting up of opportunities for interaction through organization of activities;
- being open to learning from other students' perceptions of a child, and to letting classmates have some responsibility with regard to an individual;
- acting as a model of accepting and welcoming behaviour.

Often help may come from simply standing back, watching and tactfully injecting assistance if necessary. A good example comes in the following extract of an observation of the inclusion of a boy in Year 1 (Daniel) who has joined the class as part of an inclusion project. Thomas *et al.* (1998) were observing social interaction in an inclusion project and reflect on the ease of the natural interaction that the teacher managed to facilitate. Daniel has mild physical disabilities and learning difficulties and is playing in the sand tray, when a classmate, Jo, joins him. They play in parallel for a minute or so, then …

Daniel says 'will you help me' to Jo three times. She says something and goes to help him. She pushes him out of way, gently, and makes a tunnel under his construction. After a slow start they are now talking quite frequently about their construction – she is telling him what to do and he is responding. Daniel is stereotyped in his language. Jo is making lots of imaginative comments, suggestions and directing the work in the sand. She actually gets hold of Daniel's hand to help at one point. When finished, Jo says 'Let's show Mrs X' [teacher] and Daniel calls her. The two explain it to her. Another little girl then joins the two of them. She's looking on, standing by Jo, and then moves in on the construction. The three now work together. Jo still talks to Daniel and looks for a response from him. The teacher tells the new girl to move away ... Jo has taken over the construction quite substantially now and Daniel begins to look on – albeit quite happily. Jo is chattering away. Both now move away from the sand and go over to the computer.

(Thomas *et al*. 1998: 50)

Evident here is the easy willingness of children to engage in social intercourse. In watching what the children were doing, the teacher – though it could just as easily have been a TA – held back her involvement, seeing that Daniel was getting a great deal from the interaction with Jo. Both children gained from the experience and both shared in the report which they ultimately gave to the teacher. The researchers reporting this interaction make it clear that the teacher was able skilfully to guide the report so that Daniel had his say, as indeed she had guided the sand play by unobtrusively monitoring the number of children at the tray and preventing Daniel being 'swamped' by other children.

A particularly important approach that has been introduced in recent years to promote social interaction is the *circle of friends*. Newton *et al*. (1996) give some useful suggestions on the use of circles of friends when helping the assimilation of children whose behaviour has been found difficult. Making the interesting point that using this approach is very different from a behavioural approach which would centre on ignoring difficult behaviour, they outline some features of using circles with these children. These include:

- an initial meeting with a session leader and the focus child's class (without the child present), stressing confidentiality to the class;
- comments being invited about the focus child;
- a more general discussion about relationships with the child;
- children being encouraged to think about friendships and relationships in general;
- circles being drawn showing different kinds of friendship: perhaps family, close friends and acquaintances;
- children being encouraged to reflect on what friendships and the lack of them means;

- reflections being encouraged on what no friendships means for the focus child;
- ideas being sought for helping the focus child;
- volunteers being sought who can become a circle for the focus child;
- the first meeting of the circle with the focus child being arranged.

Further ideas on professional development in this area can be obtained from the TTA's *National SEN Specialist Standards*, which can be accessed at www.tta.gov.uk/php/read.php?sectionid=100&articleid=510.

Seeing what's happening in the classroom

In 1970, the American psychologist Jacob Kounin wrote a classic text in the understanding of what happens in classrooms. The insights it has offered are as relevant today as they were when the book was written. Kounin's breakthrough was to see the classroom as an environment with an ecology, rather in the way that a habitat for plants and animals is an ecology. An ecology is a dynamic environment: if foxes are blighted, for example, rabbits do well. Or, to put it more prosaically, if you squeeze an environment in one place it bulges somewhere else.

Seeing the classroom in this way – as an ecology – Kounin said, meant that one could understand why one cannot simplistically expect to be able to impose changes without there being some consequence. His method, in coming to his conclusions, was to take extensive videotape footage of classrooms in operation. One of his main conclusions from these observations was that teachers' individual methods of discipline were less important than the overall management of the learning environment: 'it was not the way the teachers disciplined their students that was important but instead the way the classroom as a group was managed that made a difference' (1970: 180).

Kounin's findings related to the work of teachers, but they are valuable to anyone working in a classroom – teachers and assistants alike working with groups of students. Some of Kounin's key findings about this kind of management are as follows:

- It is important to be **withit** – teachers who became immersed in one issue would comment too late on the behaviour of the overall group, or may eventually pick on one child unfairly.
- It is important to be able to **overlap** – that is, to deal with two things happening at the same time – for example, to be able to deal with behaviour without interrupting work with a reading group.

- It is important to maintain **flow**, and this is done by **avoiding**:
  - **thrusts** – sudden bursting in on a group with a question or an order;
  - **deflections** from the main stream of activity – for example, making a fuss about paper on the floor when students are writing;
  - **dangles** – starting an activity and then leaving it hanging, going to something else, and then returning to the first activity;
  - **flip flops** – going back to an activity that has just been finished;
  - **overdwelling** – engaging in a stream of talk beyond that which is necessary; nagging about a certain behaviour;
  - **fragmentation** – unnecessarily asking each child in turn to do something that could be asked of the whole group;
  - **satiation** – keeping on with a topic so long that enthusiasm wanes.
- It is important to maintain group **focus** by using:
  - **alerting cues** – for example, ensuring that those children who are not at the centre of a class activity are asked questions;
  - **accountability cues** – communicated by circulating and checking.
- It is important to create **variety** in content, in both subject material and presentation.

It is interesting to note that much of Kounin's analysis distils down to the fact that successful teachers are ones who are able to cope with two things at once – able to manage the many and varied demands of the classroom. They have, if you like, developed strategies for having 'two pairs of hands', or *multi-tasking*. Many of Kounin's conclusions therefore offer powerful insights about how the work of teachers and assistants may be divided and apportioned. If 'two pairs of hands' are *actually* present, Kounin's analysis suggests how the work of managing the classroom can be divided so that the less than satisfactory solution of being obliged to multi-task is no longer necessary. If there are two people available in a classroom rather than one, then the analysis suggests how the work of these people can be intelligently shared – sharing takes the place of multi-tasking. We discuss this more in Chapter 4.

Kounin's analysis also offers important observations for reflections on our own practice, helping to 'scaffold' our own thoughts about how we might develop as teachers and TAs.

4   Three Models of Teamwork in Classrooms

In Chapters 1 and 2 we pointed to the fact that many more TAs now work in schools. Teams are therefore forming in unprecedented ways. However, as we also pointed out, there is little guidance on enhancing teamwork among these new teams in classrooms.

This is particularly disconcerting since, as the research shows, classrooms seem to provide an especially inhospitable environment for good teamwork. As we have already mentioned, team teaching, which began with high hopes in the 1960s and 1970s, encountered all kinds of problems in practice and to all intents and purposes atrophied away soon afterwards (see, e.g., Cohen 1976; Geen 1985; Hatton 1985). As we noted right at the beginning of this book, one important finding on classroom teams is that the presence of extra people in class does not automatically improve the situation for the students: having assistants in the class does not generally free the teacher for more time with the students (see, e.g., DeVault *et al.* 1977; McBrien and Weightman 1980; Thomas 1992). This finding can perhaps be explained by all of the uncertainties which are introduced when extra people work alongside the teacher.

So our aim in setting up and conducting our research was to discover methods of organizing teams in classrooms. We examined existing methods and looked also at the theoretical literature on teams to see how new team-working arrangements might best be devised.

In searching the literature on methods that might be useful in enhancing teamwork, we identified three models. Two of these, *Room Management* and *Zoning*, had originally been developed in settings other than mainstream schools. A further model, *Reflective Teamwork*, was developed especially for this study, based on the research into effective teamwork and principles from humanistic psychology.

Relevance of the three models to the tensions identified in classrooms

In Chapters 1 and 2, the literature review outlined difficulties that exist currently in teamworking arrangements in schools. In Table 4.1, these are summarized and the way that each model was intended to improve the situation is listed.

Table 4.1. Tensions in TA practice and how the models aimed to overcome these

Tension in the system	Research references		Necessary objective	Relevant models
TAs' lack of training and knowledge about classroom practice	Watkinson 1999 Clayton 1990 Lee and Mawson 1988 Farrell *et al.* 1999	→	TAs to be better informed about classroom practice and to receive training	Zoning Room Management Reflective Teamwork
TAs' concern about status	Watkinson 1999 Clayton 1990 Lee and Mawson 1998 Farrell *et al.* 1999	→	Equalize power balance between TAs and teachers and raise TA status	Reflective Teamwork
Lack of time for teachers and TAs to meet and plan together	Farrell *et al.* 1999 Lacey 1999	→	Increased opportunities to meet and plan together	Reflective Teamwork
Lack of effective teamwork between teachers and TAs	Thomas 1992 Lacey 1999	→	Improved teamwork between teachers and TAs	Reflective Teamwork
Teachers' lack knowledge of how best to work with TAs	Smith *et al.* 1999 Lee and Mawson 1988 Farrell *et al.* 1999	→	Identify and and evaluate models of TA deployment to fill this knowledge gap for teachers	Reflective Teamwork Room Management Zoning

cont.

Tension in the system	Research references		Necessary objective	Relevant models
Lack of research of TA deployment on outcome for students	Gerber *et al.* 2001 Blatchford *et al.* 2001 Roberts and Dyson 2002 Frelow *et al.* 1974 Welch *et al.* 1995	→	Evaluate the effect of different models on level of student engagement	Reflective Teamwork Room Management Zoning
Teachers deploying TAs in ways that do not promote inclusion	Bowers 1997 Thomas 1998 Hrekow and Barrow 1993 Lorenz 1998 Jones 1987 Vincett 2001 Rose 2000 French and Chopra 1999 Marks *et al.* 1999 Giangreco *et al.* 1997 Lacey 1999	→	Develop inclusive models of TA deployment	Room Management Zoning
TAs' concern about lack of clarity over their role	Watkinson 1999 Clayton 1990 Lee and Mawson 1998 Farrell *et al.* 1999	→	Provide role clarity for TAs	Room Management Zoning

The Room Management model

Given known research findings about the importance of people in a team knowing what role they are supposed to be playing, the idea behind Room Management is that each of the adults in the classroom is given a clear role. At the core of Room Management lies a period of time known as an activity period. This is a set time – for example, one hour a day – when staff undertake these specific roles.

There are two roles in the adapted system of Room Management that we employed in our research: the learning manager and the activity manager (full details of the provenance of the models begin on p. 54).

The learning manager

The learning manager concentrates on the work of individual students, working intensively with each one for short, specified periods of time. The learning manager can provide this direct teaching to any of the students in the class. If, for example, these students have special difficulties with some aspect of the curriculum, then the learning manager could provide the teaching element specified in the student's individual education plan (IEP). However, the learning manager can work with any student, not just those who have been identified as having special educational needs.

Before the session, the learning manager agrees with the activity manager which students to work with, plans the work and assembles the materials needed for each student. During the session, the learning manager works with these students individually in turn.

The activity manager

The activity manager supports the rest of the students in the class (i.e. those not being taught by the learning manager). These students are typically arranged into groups, and the main aim of the activity manager is to keep them engaged on the task in hand. The 'teaching' is planned to be less intensive because of the larger task of managing the main body of the class.

Work can therefore be planned for these students on areas of the curriculum that have already been taught, though not necessarily mastered. Students will therefore be consolidating on material and should require less individual help from the activity manager. Before the session, tasks, activities and materials are organized for each group of students.

During the session the activity manager ensures that each group has appropriate materials, books and equipment. The activity manager moves around the groups and will, for example, prompt students to start working if necessary, praise students who are busy and give feedback on their work. The support is at a less intensive level than that provided by the learning manager. The activity manager also manages the routine and control of the class, dealing with any interruptions. This frees up the learning manager to provide individual teaching without distraction.

The roles of activity and learning manager can be allocated in a number of different ways depending on the preferences of the personnel involved, the organization of the classroom and the needs of the students. If there are more than two adults in the classroom, then there may be more than one learning manager or activity manager. During the session staff may switch roles – for example, the one who was the learning manager during the first part could become the activity manager for the latter part.

Theory underpinning Room Management

Room Management arose out of the work of Hart and Risley (1976) and has been used in a variety of settings for adults and students with serious physical and learning difficulties (Porterfield *et al.* 1977; Coles and Blunden 1979; McBrien and Weightman 1980). In the UK, Room Management was included in the Education of the Developmentally Young (EDY) project (see McBrien and Weightman 1980 for a description of the work undertaken at the Hester Adrian Centre, University of Manchester.

The aim of Room Management is to enable the teacher to meet the learning needs of individual students while at the same time keeping the larger group engaged. It is these conflicting demands on teachers that it is so difficult to reconcile. For example, Brophy (1982) in a meta-analysis of research into classroom management found that successful teachers are able to attend to the learning needs of individuals as well as to techniques for group management. He found a tension in the teacher's role between providing for individuals and maintaining contact with the class as a whole. Similarly, the ORACLE study (Galton *et al.* 1980) found that one of the most difficult features of successful classroom management is the ability to reconcile individual teaching with group engagement. Doyle (1986) also found that the central professional challenge facing the teacher with limited and finite resources of attention, time and energy is how to organize the class to balance the keeping of order (in the sense of managing classrooms, events, resources and movement) at the same time as attending to individual students' learning.

Room Management helps the teacher attend to these two competing demands, by enabling additional adults to take on elements of the teacher's role. To put it simply, one person concentrates on intensive teaching of individual students while the other concentrates on keeping the rest of the students purposefully engaged.

The ability meet the learning needs of individual students

In Chapter 3 we indicated that learning takes place when it is:

- in a stress-free situation;
- at the right level;
- in regular, small doses;
- provided with plenty of help;
- fun;
- rewarding.

For these needs to be met, the teacher needs to provide students with some individual or small-group input, even if this is of very short duration. One clear aim of Room Management procedures is to increase the amount of direct teaching to individual students, undertaken by the learning manager.

Reconciling disparate classroom priorities

In the well-known classroom observation study which went under the acronym of ORACLE, Galton *et al.* (1980) demonstrated that there are aspects of classroom pedagogy and management that it is very difficult to reconcile. It is difficult to keep the main body of the class engaged while at the same time providing a lot of individual teaching. ORACLE found that teachers who were good at providing individual teaching were not necessarily so good at keeping the rest of the class engaged. The converse was also true; teachers who were good at keeping most of the class working were not so effective in providing individual teaching.

Good teachers find ways of reconciling the difficulties of providing individual or small-group help at the same time as managing the class. They do this by, for example, using the *overlapping* which Kounin (1970) described, and which we outlined in Chapter 3. Nevertheless, even if one has developed these multi-tasking strategies to a high degree, it is still a difficult thing to achieve.

Having additional people in the classroom offers possibilities for reconciling these difficulties further, by enabling the differentiation of activities, with each person fulfilling a specialized role. In Room Management the activity manager concentrates on keeping on task all those students who are not being provided with individual teaching, while the learning manager concentrates on the intensive teaching.

An adaptation of the Room Management model

The original principles for Room Management suggested that the learning manager would work intensively with individual students for short, specified periods of time. Concern was expressed by the teachers during the first training session that this role would not sit easily with the organization of the groupwork part of the Literacy Hour – National Literacy Strategy guidelines encouraged teachers to create five groups and each day work intensively with two.

The usual interpretation of this advice was for the teacher to work with one group and the TA to work with the other. The three remaining groups would work independently on tasks set by the teacher. An alternative under the Room Management framework would be for the learning manager to work intensively with one group and the activity manager to monitor the work of the other four groups. Our adaptation therefore allowed for the option of the learning manager working intensively with one group as a *group* rather than as a series of individuals.

The Zoning model

Zoning refers to a system of classroom organization where adults take responsibility for different geographical areas or *zones* of the classroom.

The idea behind Zoning is that clarity – about who is doing what – is provided by clear definition as to where in the classroom different people are working. Thus, looking at Figure 4.1, one person will be responsible, for example, for groups A, B, C and D while another will be responsible for groups E and F. The adult responsible for each group needs to change regularly.

Issues when adopting Zoning include how students are grouped during the session and whether this is the same as normal or whether there is a rearrangement for the purposes of the session. The balance of the groups in each zone also needs to be considered – for example:

- Will the grouped zones comprise the same students as normally sit in these places, or will there be a rearrangement for the purpose of the session?
- What will be the balance of the groups? 4/2 (as in the example) or 3/3?
- What will be the balance of the groups to the teacher/TA? Will the teacher take the larger group while the TA takes the smaller group?
- Will the students with special needs be placed in groups being overseen by the TA or the teacher?

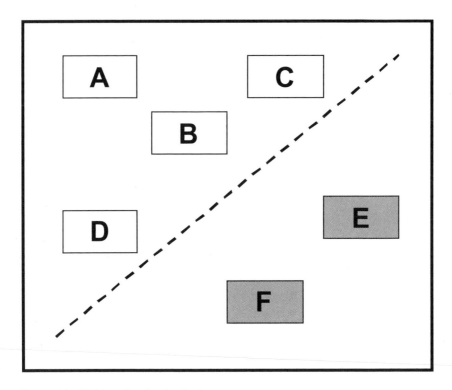

Figure 4.1. Division of a class by Zoning

Theory underpinning Zoning

The Zoning model is very simple. Adults are allocated to areas of the class-room based on the physical arrangement of the room. Different activities will be occurring in different parts of the classroom and so adults will take responsibility for the activity in that particular area. Anecdotally, it is often said that nursery classes are organized using Zoning principles, so for example one person may take responsibility for the book corner, another for students on the painting table and so on.

The model assumes a strong link between the geography of the class-room and how students learn most effectively. Zoning assumes that out-comes for students have been clearly defined and that particular types of layout will enable these to be met. For example, if the objectives are for students to learn to collaborate and communicate with each other, then they would best be seated in groups. If students are doing individual tasks, then they should be working on their own, because in groups it is easier to get distracted. (It is worth noting in this regard that research – e.g. Tann 1988; Wheldall 1988 – tends to suggest this matching of setting to needs does not generally occur, so that even when teachers want students to be doing individual tasks they tend to place them in groups.)

A study by Thomas (1985) of a classroom of 10- and 11-year-old students looked at how much students were on task. He found that those children who were sitting on their own or at the periphery of the classroom activity were, in general, more on task than those who were in groups. In fact, those children sitting on their own had migrated *away* from groups – presumably to avoid distraction – by their own choice, not by teacher direction. A further finding was that those who were in groups had roughly similar on-task levels.

Grouping of students is a very commonly observed classroom layout in primary schools and the justification is to foster communication, cooperation and imagination, usually through groupwork. However, observational research (e.g. Bennett and Blundell 1983) suggests that students are often being asked to do *individual* work in groups. The very features of groups which make them good for cooperation and communication make them poor for doing individual work. Students do individual work best in a setting which minimizes distraction. Weinstein (1979), in a major review of classroom research, cites a case-study which compared two classrooms which were similar in all but classroom geography. In classroom A, desks were arranged so that only two or three children could work together; areas for different activities were set apart by barriers such as bookcases, and areas for quiet study for activities were also set apart; the teacher's desk was in the corner so that she was unable to direct activities from it and had to move around the room a great deal. Here, conversation was quieter, and the children were more engaged, with longer attention spans than those in classroom B. In classroom B, large groups of children (up to 12) were supposed to be working together (despite the individualized curriculum). Areas for different activities were not clearly designated and the teacher's desk was centrally located, enabling her to direct activity from her seat.

There is evidence that children prefer classrooms not organized in the traditional format with groups. Pfluger and Zola (1974), for instance, found that children preferred a large space in the centre of the room, with furniture along the walls. Children may even prefer being in formal rows rather than being in groups (see, e.g., Wheldall *et al.* 1981; Bennett and Blundell 1983).

Delefes and Jackson (1972) found that an 'action zone' exists in many classrooms. Most of the teacher's interactions occur with students at the front and in the middle of the class, even in classrooms which in theory have no front. Saur *et al.* (1984) found that hearing-impaired children sitting at the periphery of the class are doubly disadvantaged. Withdrawn or poorly motivated students might also be doubly disadvantaged by the existence of such a zone.

The Zoning model encourages thinking about the geography of the classroom, the grouping of the children, the location of adults in the classroom and the placement of certain students to meet their needs appropriately. Further ideas on how to consider classroom arrangements and the use of adults in those arrangements can be found in Chapters 8 and 9 in Part 2 of this book.

The Reflective Teamwork model

The aim of Room Management and Zoning is to enhance teamwork by making expected activity clearer for team participants – what is known in the teamwork literature as *role clarity*. These two models of management reduce ambiguity for team participants about what they should be doing. They specify very clearly what participants should be doing and where they should be doing it, and in the case of Room Management there is also a pedagogic rationale that underlies this role specification.

The aim of Reflective Teamwork, by contrast, is to improve classroom teamwork by enhancing communication, planning and review.

In our research, pairs of teachers and TAs were trained to improve their skills of working together, particularly skills of effective communication. During the six-week intervention, the teacher-TA pairs were asked to meet daily for 15 minutes and to follow a structure to plan and review their teaching sessions in full collaboration, as equal partners. The 15-minute planning meeting started with a review of the previous session (except of course for the very first meeting). The TA identified two things that had gone well during the session, followed by two things that could be improved upon. The TA then expressed how they were feeling by completing the sentence 'I am feeling ... because'. While the TA spoke, the teacher listened actively, adopting an open posture, maintaining good eye contact and asking questions, putting into practice the skills of effective communication that were made explicit during training sessions. After the TA had finished, the teacher summarized what had been expressed.

The teacher then listed two things that had gone well and two things that could be improved upon, again expressing their feelings and reasoning. The TA listened actively and then summarized what the teacher had said.

The meeting then turned to planning for the next teaching session. The teacher and TA brainstormed together objectives and activities, which were then evaluated jointly. These were agreed upon and written up. Table 4.2 shows the structure for the 15-minute planning meeting.

Table 4.2. The structure of the planning session in Reflective Teamwork

Review of previous session

Minutes	Who	Content
2	TA	Two things that went well
	TA	Two things that we could improve
	TA	I am feeling … because …
1	Teacher	Summarize four things and feelings
2	Teacher	Two things that went well
	Teacher	Two things that we could improve
	Teacher	I am feeling … because …
1	TA	Summarize four things and feelings

Plan next session

Minutes	Who	Content	
3	TA/teacher together	Brainstorm	Objectives
			Activities
3		Evaluate objectives and activities	
3		Agree and write up plan	

Theory underpinning the Reflective Teamwork model

The model is underpinned by theory and research of various kinds.

Humanistic psychology

The model has its roots in humanistic psychology, which developed out of the writings of Rogers (1951) and Maslow (1962). Humanistic psychology implies that human beings are complex and capable of exercising choice, rather than being victims of past experience. It contains as a guiding principle the idea that the individual possesses a natural ability to develop to their full potential, a process that Maslow called 'self-actualization'.

Humanistic counselling

The model is based on humanistic counselling, which relies on the quality of the relationship between one person and another. The humanistic counsellor shows 'unconditional positive regard' (Rogers 1951) for people. Thus, advice and judgement will be avoided. People gain clarity about a problem, have feelings validated and accepted, and move on to create options for future action. Humanistic counselling involves acceptance, active listening and the development of rapport and empathy.

The Reflective Teamwork model is based on humanistic counselling in that the teacher and the TA develop their relationship through a genuine desire to communicate, with rapport and empathy, and with unconditional acceptance of the other's feelings about the teaching of students in their class. Counselling skills are used when the teacher or TA gives the other a designated amount of uninterrupted listening time and when the listener reflects back feelings and summarizes what the speaker has said. As in counselling, the summary serves both to clarify meaning and to enhance feelings of rapport and self-esteem.

Self-esteem

Coopersmith (1967) has defined self-esteem as a personal judgement of worthiness. Reflective teamwork aims to enhance the self-esteem of teachers and TAs through opportunities to have their feelings and perspectives accepted unconditionally by the other. There is no requirement that the other shares, or even agrees with, these feelings and perspectives. Acceptance merely implies the right of any individual to have their own unique thoughts and feelings in a given situation.

Locus of control

Perhaps the strongest link between Reflective Teamwork and humanistic psychology is the notion of the 'client-centred' approach (Rogers 1951) and locus of control. The development of an internal locus of control has been shown to be directly related to the attribution made by the individual as to what was responsible for success or failure in a given situation (Phares 1957).

Reflective Teamwork aims to use structured meeting and planning time to generate options for solving problems that the team has identified.

Cooperation and social interdependence

An essential aspect of cooperation is developing trust among group members. Group effectiveness relies on every member sharing resources, giving and receiving help, dividing the work, and contributing to the team goals. Group members will more openly express their thoughts, feelings, reactions, opinions, information and ideas when the trust level is high (Deutsch 1973).

A key issue for teams of teachers and TAs is the difference in status, pay, training, qualifications and responsibilities of the members of the classroom teams, which is likely to effect cooperation and trust between members. As Lacey (2001: 102) notes, though, 'status becomes of little importance if everyone has a role that is particular to them and they are appreciated when they carry it out'. Her research suggested that teachers experience the most difficulties when they are unsure of the role of the TA.

There have been many studies looking at the effect of power in teams. Johnson and Johnson (2000) found that the effectiveness of groups improves when power is relatively balanced among the members, and when power is based on competence, expertise and information. The ability of groups to solve problems increases as all team members come to believe that they share equally in influencing the direction of the group effort and as the group climate becomes relatively free of the domination by a few of the most powerful members. When members have equal power they are more cooperative in their interactions, more responsive to other members and more committed to implementing the group decision. Studies have found that within organizations the satisfaction of subordinates increases when they believe they can influence particular aspects of the organization's decision-making (Tjosvold 1991). Unequal power interferes with the trust and communication necessary for managing group conflicts constructively. Thus, the problem-solving ability of a group is improved when the group has dynamic power patterns that re-equalize influence among group members. A real issue for classroom teams is how to promote equality and trust when members have different status. The Reflective Teamwork model aims to equalize the power balance between teachers and TAs.

Effective communication and meetings

Communication has been identified as a vital ingredient of effective teamwork. Rainforth *et al.* (1992) suggest that interaction is particularly important when teams are first set up. Katzenbach and Smith (1993) found that successful teams gave themselves time to learn to be a team and that the first meeting was particularly important in setting the tone for the future.

Much of the literature on effective communication focuses on the importance of being clear about the messages you are sending, and active listening. Johnson and Johnson (2000) demonstrate that team members can be taught the interpersonal and small-group skills needed for high-quality cooperation, including getting to know and trust each other, communicating accurately and unambiguously, accepting and supporting each other and resolving conflicts constructively. They stress the need for 'frequent and regular meetings that provide opportunities for team members to interact face to face and promote each other's success' (2000: 553).

The importance of face-to-face meetings between teachers and TAs is highly relevant to the effectiveness of classroom teams. Johnson and Johnson (2000) have shown that communication is affected by the status of members. They suggest actively pursuing equal participation of all members and the promotion of valuing of all members' ideas and views, regardless of status. This issue is relevant to teacher-TA teams where the TAs generally have lower status than the teachers. The 15-minute planning meeting gives equal talking time to the teacher and the TA.

Empowerment and problem-solving

As we noted in Chapter 2, the ability of teams to experience autonomy and to engage in problem-solving is crucially important. The Reflective Teamwork model encouraged teachers and TA teams to identify and to solve their own problems, thereby encouraging autonomy and empowerment of the team. During the daily 15-minute planning meetings, teachers and TAs were asked to solve problems by brainstorming alternatives and evaluating the advantages and disadvantages of each.

Regular reviews

There is evidence that teams function more effectively if they regularly review how well they are doing (Garvin 1988). Sundstrom *et al.* (1990) suggest teams should review both team performance and team viability, including team member satisfaction, participation and willingness to continue working together. The need for regular reviews was included in the framework for the TA and teacher daily 15-minute meetings. Classteachers and TA teams began these meetings by reflecting on how successful the previous teaching session had been and how this had made them feel.

Reflective practice

Reflective practice is described briefly on p. 33. Many have written about reflective practice, but perhaps its most articulate advocate has been Donald Schön. In his book *The Reflective Practitioner: How Professionals Think in Action* (1991) Schön argues eloquently for many fields of professional practice needing to examine their *know-how* knowledge, rather than their *know-what* knowledge. Teaching, Schön says, is an art, where practitioners learn by doing.

It is the aspect of reflectivity that is important here, and the assumption behind our model of Reflective Teamwork is that reflectivity – in the sense that Schön means it – among team members is essential for the success of the team.

Original research into the three models

Room Management

McBrien and Weightman (1980) undertook research on the EDY project. This was a behavioural approach to teaching students with profound and multiple learning difficulties. As part of the EDY project, staff were taught behaviour modification techniques, but were not able to use these effectively because the average classroom in a school for children with severe learning difficulties did not provide regular opportunities for one-to-one teaching. This was due to the short length of the school day and the amount of time spent on routine maintenance activities, including toileting, feeding and dressing. Even with a ratio of three staff to nine students, contact time in terms of teaching was very low.

The aim of the research was to organize more time during the school day for one-to-one teaching without detriment to the rest of the students in the class group. The study focused on seven students, all with profound and multiple learning difficulties. The developmental levels of these students ranged from 1–12 months on a variety of developmental checks.

Adults were given training in the roles identified under Room Management. These included a 'room manager', who was responsible for all students except those receiving individual work. Duties included checking that students had the right equipment, then moving quickly from student to student, spending a few seconds on each student and prompting those who were off task, or praising those students on task. The room manager did not toilet children or mop up or leave the room until relieved. A second role was that of the individual worker who taught a list of individual students one at a time. A third role was that of the mover, who had the task of toileting students, moving large pieces of equipment and students at the request of the room manager and dealing with all emergencies, including spillages and visitors, the aim being to keep the room manager free of all distractions. The teacher discussed these roles with her assistants and planned a timetable such that Room Management took place for 45 minutes each day. During the 45 minute period, each of the three adults spent 15 minutes in each role, the order being changed daily.

A baseline-intervention-baseline (ABA) design was used with a training period for staff taking place following the first baseline. Each condition was carried out for 45–60 minutes daily for one week. At the start of the study adults were given a training and feedback week, during which the room manager's behaviour was monitored by one of the research team. Feedback in the form of verbal prompts and positive reinforcement was given during the practice sessions. During the intervention period, Room Management was carried out as in the practice week but no training was given. Then followed a return to baseline period, during which staff were asked to return to their usual method of working and not to practice Room Management procedures. The same procedures were followed for these baselines as for the initial baseline.

Data were collected on the engagement levels of students and also on the Room Management behaviour. Engagement data were recorded for each individual student separately according to criteria for each student because there were large individual differences in the class.

Every minute each student was observed in a predetermined order and a check made on the data sheet. Each minute was concluded by writing down the number of adults in the room. The percentage engagement levels were calculated by dividing the number of on-task tallies by the total number of observations. Analysis showed that the mean engagement levels of the group rose significantly under the Room Management procedures compared to either baseline.

Data were also collected on the individual attention that students received from an adult. Attention could be of any kind, (e.g. changing a nappy, carrying, prompting or providing rewards). Findings suggested that Room Management changed the quality of attention given to students by adults in such a way as to increase their engagement.

While McBrien and Weightman conducted their research in a special school, Thomas (1985) assessed Room Management procedures in a mainstream classroom. Twenty-one students in Year 6, aged 10 to 11 years, were observed.

Normal practice was for the students to work independently from written material and to ask the teacher for clarification or to have work marked. For some sessions a TA was also available who supported one or two particular students. Parents provided help in the classroom, usually working with their own students.

The team involved in the study comprised a teacher, a TA and two parents. Procedures for Room Management were introduced with one individual helper and three activity managers responsible for four groups of six students. For the hour that the Room Management ran, the teacher took on the role of individual helper, focusing on two particular students, while the other adults worked as activity managers, concentrating on maintaining the focus of groups of students.

Data were collected on the engagement level of each student in the class – a simple on/off dichotomy. Videotape recordings were made of the group under three conditions. The first condition (baseline) involved the classroom functioning normally with one teacher and one TA but without parents. In the second condition the same classroom functioned with two parents. In the third condition the classroom functioned under Room Management procedures with the same two parents. Video recordings were made for one hour of students under each condition, each student in the class being observed for 6 minutes. Results were therefore based on a total of 6 hours 18 minutes of observation. Recordings were made on the same day of the week and at the same times. As far as it was possible to control for this, the students were therefore doing the same sort of activity on each recording. The videos were analysed by sampling every ten seconds for each student whether they were on- or off-task. Criteria for on- and off-task were based on the Becker *et al.* (1967) categories. The mean engagement level for each child was calculated and a repeated measures design was used, comparing each child with him- or herself across the conditions.

Analysis of the data showed clear differences existing at baseline (no parents) and the two conditions where parents were helping. The mean engagement of the group rose from around 60 per cent at baseline, to around 70 per cent when the parents were present, to over 80 per cent when organized according to the Room Management procedures. The greatest difference existed between the baseline and the parents with Room Management. Significant differences were found to exist between baseline and parents without Room Management and between parents without Room Management and where Room Management was used. The system affected most beneficially the engagement of those students who initially had the lowest on-task behaviour.

Zoning

Le Laurin and Risley (1972) were concerned with improving the way that children move from one activity to another in preschool settings, since prior research had shown that without clear guidelines children can become distracted as they change activity (Gump 1969).

The study compared two different models for assigning adult responsibility to children as they moved between activities – the Zoning and 'man to man' procedures. In the man-to-man method, the teacher supervised a group of specific children, who were kept together in each activity so that the first child waited for the last to finish. When the last child was finished, the teacher presented the next activity so that all the children faced the new activity at the same time. The Zoning method involved teachers being assigned responsibility to a particular activity area and for those children passing through it. As each child finished an activity he or she was sent directly to another activity area and another teacher.

The two methods were compared in terms of the amount of time that children were engaged in teacher-planned activities during the transition from lunch to nap activities each day in a nursery facility taking children with an age range of 3 to 5 years. Daily attendance was 26 to 43 children (average of 39). There were three full-time teachers and one headteacher/administrator.

Measures of group participation were used to compare how much of a child's time was lost from planned activities during the daily transition from lunch, through the bathroom and dressing areas, to the nap area.

Data were collected during the lunch to nap transition by five trained observers located in the lunch area, bathroom, shoe area and bed area. The fifth observer took reliability observations in one randomly assigned area each day throughout the study. Starting at precisely the same time, observers first counted the total number of children, recorded it, then counted the total number of children engaged in activities, and recorded that. Counts were begun at the beginning of each 60-second interval.

The staff in the centre had used the man-to-man procedure since the centre opened. The Zoning procedure was introduced, then baseline data were taken for six days. The staff then returned to the man-to-man procedure for seven days.

Findings suggested that the Zoning method led to shorter transitions and a higher level of child engagement, while the man-to-man method was typified by longer transitions with a lower level of child engagement. The study clearly demonstrates the effectiveness with which the Zoning procedure accomplished lunch to nap-time transition.

Reflective Teamwork

Reflective Teamwork is a system as yet untrialled, and its development for the projects reported in this book rests on a range of research, some of which was referred to in Chapter 2.

It is also worth noting that Johnson and Johnson (2000) reviewed over 520 experimental and over 100 correlational research studies comparing cooperative, competitive and individualistic efforts. They found that the degree of cooperation and positive interdependence within a team impacted upon effort to achieve, positive relationships, psychological adjustment and social competence. Positive interdependence among group members resulted in their encouraging and facilitating each other's efforts to produce, seeking more information from each other, utilizing each other's information, engaging in oral rehearsal of the information being exchanged, and influencing each other's attitudes and conclusions. In comparison with competitive groups and individuals, cooperative team members were more intrinsically motivated to succeed, strove harder for mutual benefit and had greater motivation to persist and complete the task. Interestingly for the research in hand, while cooperation tends to promote higher achievement and productivity, Johnson and Johnson found that its superiority over competitive and individualistic approaches is most clearly seen in conceptually complex and problem-solving tasks such as those faced by teachers and TAs in meeting the needs of students with special needs.

Goleman (1998) quotes research carried out by Drukat comparing the competencies of the ten most outstanding teams in a large American factory with those of ten average ones doing the same job. The 'star teams' had the following competencies: empathy, or interpersonal understanding; cooperation and a unified effort; open communication, setting explicit norms and expectations, and confronting underperforming team members; a drive to improve, so that the team paid attention to performance feedback and sought to learn to do better; self-awareness, in the form of evaluating their strengths and weaknesses as a team; initiative and taking a proactive stance towards problem-solving; self-confidence as a team; flexibility in how they went about their collective tasks; organizational awareness, in terms of both assessing the needs of other key groups in the company and being resourceful in using what the organization had to offer; building bonds to other teams.

Overview

In this chapter, the three models of Room Management, Zoning and Reflective Teamwork have been outlined and their origins and contexts described. The Room Management research review reveals that this method of organizing the adults in a classroom has potential for increasing the engagement levels of the students and the role clarity of the staff. The limited research on Zoning suggests that it is a potentially highly successful method of assigning adult responsibility for children during transitions. This method may have applications for allocating adult resources in class-rooms. Reflective Teamwork has not yet been trialled as a system, though – as we have tried to indicate – there is strong theoretical justification for employing it.

Room Management and Zoning are prescriptive about the roles and responsibilities of staff during the teaching session. Reflective Teamwork is different in that while it is prescriptive about how frequently teachers and TAs should meet and how they should conduct meetings, they then decide together how they deploy their joint resources in class.

In the following chapter the research that we conducted into these three methods is described.

5 Action Research into the Models – Phase 1

There were two phases of research. In the first, six primary schools volunteered to become involved in the project, and we asked these schools each to take on one of the models described in Chapter 4. The evaluation would comprise teacher and TA feedback, as well as structured observation of students' behaviour in the classroom.

Thus, two of the schools were asked to undertake Room Management, two were asked to undertake Zoning, and two were asked to undertake Reflective Teamwork. The findings helped us to understand how the models worked and to analyse the strengths and weaknesses of each.

By the time we were ready to conduct the second phase of the research a year later, we had learned lessons from the findings of Phase 1 and the feedback of those colleagues who had participated at that stage. On the basis of these findings and this feedback, new, more adaptive models were devised and these were evaluated using more flexible, user-orientated methods.

We also listened to the feedback of secondary schools in Essex who had heard of the findings relating to Phase 1, and who had asked that we should extend the research to the secondary sector.

The full details of the first phase of the research are given in this and the following chapter. Details of the second phase are given in Chapter 7.

Research setting, issues and questions

The first question to be answered in our research was 'What is the effect of each model, when adopted, on the engagement of the students in the class when it is used?' and the second question, 'How far do staff members (teachers and teaching assistants) assess the consequences of adoption of these models on their own effectiveness in providing good teaching and/or support?' Additional questions arising from this second question arose about possible adaptations that could be made to the models to improve their effectiveness.

With these questions in mind, our evaluation of the models outlined in Chapter 4 centred on two kinds of outcome:

- student engagement
- staff members' perceptions and assessments of their own effectiveness in management and pedagogy when using the models.

The six schools were identified from the Essex inclusive schools project, these schools receiving extra funding from the DfES via the LEA to look at an element of inclusive practice within their schools. Each school, named with a pseudonym in Table 5.1, was asked to identify one class to be actively involved in the research.

Table 5.1. Intervention models and year group of classes

Research model	Year group	School (all primary schools)
Room Management	Y3	Mableton
Room Management	Y2	Goldthorpe
Zoning	Y3	Benfield
Zoning	Y2	Tilsley
Reflective Teamwork	Y3	Crickwood
Reflective Teamwork	Y2	Larch

The teacher/assistant pair from each school received half a day's training on the relevant model. This was followed up three weeks later by another half day, which provided the participants with an opportunity to clarify issues that had arisen and to solve any problems.

Each school was asked to implement its model for a period of six weeks and to introduce the relevant model for one session each week. Schools were asked to implement the model during the groupwork part of the Literacy Hour. The intervention period began immediately after the training had finished.

Method

As noted above, the three models were evaluated on the basis of structured observation and feedback from participants in each school. Throughout, the work was small-scale and action research orientated, focusing on changes in specific situations. While elements of this research design have adopted methods appropriate to systematic study in such situations (i.e., using repeated measures design relating to students' engagement, see below), it has also been characteristic of this project to work closely with the schools as findings emerged seeking adaptation and improvement to the models as appropriate. Thus, detailed feedback on the workings of each model was sought from the participants in the project in individual and group interviews.

Structured observation

Mean engagement levels for each student in each classroom were obtained and a repeated measures design used, comparing each student with him- or herself, the comparison occurring between engagement before and at the end of the intervention. In other words, application of the independent variable – the use of the models – interrupted subsequent measurement of the dependent variable – students' engagement – and differences in the data series before and after the interruption were examined to determine whether or not the independent variable caused the dependent variable (engagement) to vary.

A pre-intervention measure of the level of engagement of all the students in the six classes was obtained by videotaping all the students in each of the six classes. Each class was videoed during the groupwork part of the Literacy Hour before the teachers and assistants were provided with any training on the intervention models. Wide-angle video cameras were set up in each classroom on a high tripod so that all students in the class could be seen. The classes were taped for the whole of the Literacy Hour, so that by the time the 20-minute groupwork started the students had had the opportunity of acclimatizing to the cameras. Once filming had started, the camera operators left the classrooms. Each classroom was then videoed again at the end of the six-week period of implementing the models.

The videotapes were then analysed, with the focus on each student in turn, to determine his or her level of engagement every ten seconds for a period of ten minutes during the groupwork section of the Literacy Hour. For this purpose a simple on-off task measure was used. Categories for on-task/off-task were devised on the basis of the Becker *et al.* (1967) categories for behaviour incompatible with learning (off-task) and relevant behaviour (on-task).

Interviews

Data were collected on the perceptions of the teachers and assistants in relation to joint planning, teamwork and role clarity and how the intervention was different to their previous practice. Data were obtained using semi-structured interviews and group interviews.

For the semi-structured individual interviews all six teachers and five of the six TAs were interviewed individually (one assistant being unavailable).

The interviews were conducted at the end of the period of intervention of the models.

The following foci were stressed during the interviews:

- information on how the principles outlined at the training sessions were put into practice in the classroom;
- views on how the intervention affected teamworking, planning arrangements and role clarity of the teachers and TAs;
- views on the effects on children;
- reflections on how the model was different from customary practice.

For the group interviews the personnel operating each particular method were brought together for discussion with the aim of identifying variations, idiosyncrasies and adaptations in the operation of the models and as a means of sharing good practice. Thus the first group comprised teachers and TAs operating Reflective Teamwork; the second group comprised those operating Room Management, while the third group comprised those operating Zoning.

Documentary evidence

Teachers and TAs kept documentary records showing how the interventions were implemented – these included planning sheets for the Literacy Hour and for Zoning and Room Management. The teamwork group were asked to keep brief notes of their meetings.

Findings

Observational analysis

Findings of the repeated measures studies are given in Figures 5.1 to 5.6, which show the baseline engagement for each student alongside post-intervention engagement figures; students are ordered in each class by their baseline engagement. The findings are summarized in Table 5.2, which shows that in all classes there were significant improvements in students' engagement between the baseline and experimental conditions.

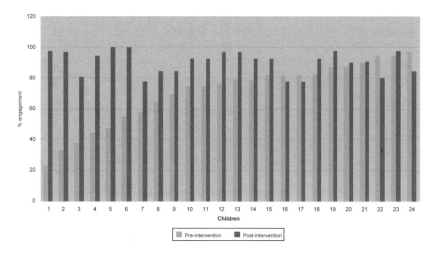

Figure 5.1 Room Management at Mableton

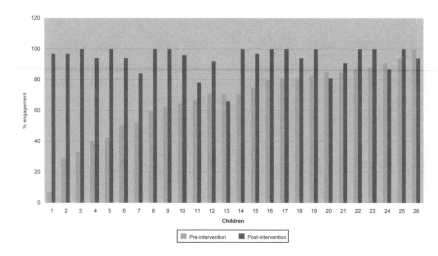

Figure 5.2 Room Management at Goldthorpe

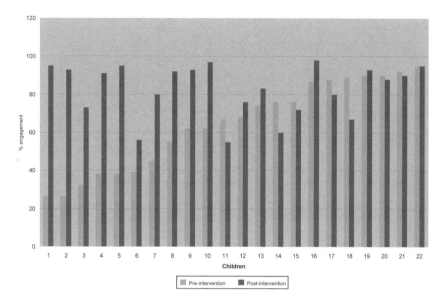

Figure 5.3 Zoning at Benfield

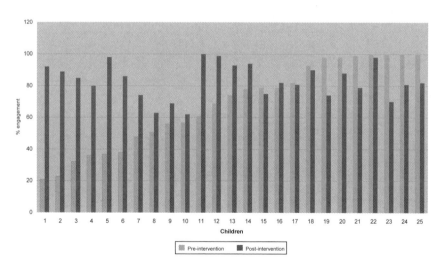

Figure 5.4 Zoning at Tilsley

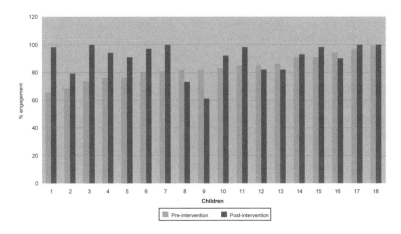

Figure 5.5 Reflective Teamwork at Crickwood

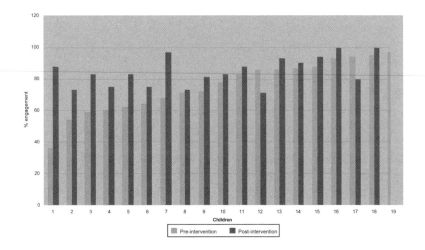

Figure 5.6 Reflective Teamwork at Larch

Table 5.2 Changes in engagement between baseline and implementation

Model	Figure	Mean change %	P(T<=t) two tail
Room Management (Mableton)	5.1	19.9	0.0004
Room Management (Goldthorpe)	5.2	26.6	<0.0001
Zoning (Benfield)	5.3	18.5	0.0046
Zoning (Tilsley)	5.4	13.7	0.0286
Reflective Teamwork (Crickwood)	5.5	7.4	0.0298
Reflective Teamwork (Larch)	5.6	9.8	0.0113

These findings are discussed in detail in 'Comments on Phase 1', on p. 72–3.

Interviews and focus groups

The findings of the analysis of the qualitative data (interviews and focus groups) are reported here.

Room Management

In Goldthorpe, the TA was given the role of activity manager. She enjoyed this role, although she felt uncomfortable at first 'taking charge' of the class while the teacher was in the room. She felt that the children stayed on task, but that they lacked her 'personal attention'.

The teacher in Goldthorpe was doubtful about the value of the approach from the outset. His main concern was to avoid the activity manager being responsible for too many children. He therefore decided that the TA should work only with groups, not with individual students. He was also concerned about melding the approach with the Literacy strategy, although in practice there were several points of consonance, with the role of the learning manager being similar to the role of the teacher in the standard Literacy Hour format. Indeed, an advantage that became apparent as the Room Management research progressed was that the learning manager was able to concentrate on the target group with few interruptions.

Other problems encountered by the teacher in Goldthorpe were the time involved in producing detailed planning sheets and the rise in noise level when he was focusing his attention on one group. By the end of week two he had established a programme of 'visiting' (cf. 'roaming' from Zoning) groups:

I felt that each time I visited a group I could talk about an additional aspect of their task and set them a further task and extend the original task a bit at a time. They then had time to carry out what we discussed before I came back to them. The 'visiting' seemed to set a timetable by which they had to have completed or at least started the extension task. I preferred this way of doing literacy: I think that the learning targets are achieved better this way.

Another problem encountered involved teacher and children's perceptions of the role of the TA.

From my point of view, the role of the activity manager is the most contentious one. If an assistant assumes this role, then surely it is asking far too much of her for her to take on responsibility for the learning of this number of children. If the teacher assumes this role, then it would seem that circulating around the classroom prompting individual children and offering praise is far removed from the role of the teacher in the National Literacy Strategy.

The teacher at Mableton felt that children got the hang of Room Management very quickly, and that it led to more groups of children receiving support and guidance. In particular, she felt that children were more responsive to support from the TA, and that these processes encouraged them to respect and value her guidance more. Room Management encouraged independence in the children, with children of lower ability benefiting from not being seen as the only group in receipt of additional support. Room Management also systematized the 'teaching' element, enabling greater communication and shared understanding between the teacher and the TA through more detailed planning. The teacher felt encouraged to reflect more on 'how I supported the special needs through the assistant', and these processes encouraged the two adults to complement one another more. There were negative aspects of this increased teamworking though, in the more intensive time implication.

Zoning

The TA at Benfield described how the system evolved, as time was needed to arrive at the best way of configuring the groups. It took a week for a stable pattern of groups-to-staff to emerge. Questions arose concerning the demands of certain of the groups, and whether it was possible to manage two more demanding groups together. Once a system had been found, zones tended to take the same pattern each week, with some thought as to a different Zoning pattern at the beginning of literacy sessions to ensure that each group was heard on a regular basis.

The TA felt empowered by the Zoning process, and more effective as a result: 'I found that Zoning helped me feel more able to do things in the class without always asking the teacher, so I felt more responsible for my area and the children in it'. Likewise the teacher felt that Zoning 'seemed a natural way to organize the classroom. It is easier to monitor students' work and behaviour, and it utilizes the TA more effectively.'

The children took a little time to understand the subtleties of Zoning. At first they went to whoever was available and had to be reminded of the new rules. To reinforce this system of working, the TA and the teacher decided to 'roam' between the tables, rather than being more static at one, and this seemed to solve the problem.

The teacher at Benfield generally felt that Zoning was a successful strategy 'Zoning generally releases the teacher to get on with teaching one small group, while two other groups are being catered for, and the two other groups are working independently. It has meant that the poorer ones have been able to receive greater help.'

The notion of 'enforcing', raised by the teacher at Benfield, is an interesting one. The teacher noted that Zoning may be particularly useful when extra people are coming into the class to help (e.g. parents). A parent, say, can be allocated a group, and the teacher can take the role of 'enforcer' to bring direction and discipline.

At Tilsley, Zoning was used principally to enable mixed-ability teaching. The TA felt that Zoning was good for inclusion, since the less able children were integrated within the whole class, rather than being seen as a separate group. All children got attention more quickly, as fewer congregated on one adult – usually the teacher. This resulted in more children tending to be on-task, with resulting improved behaviour.

The teacher at Tilsley also felt that Zoning successfully facilitated mixed-ability teaching, and that it worked best when the task was the same with differentiation by outcome/expectation. It helped those students who needed role models of more positive behaviour to learn from their peers, and enabled other children to begin to develop 'helping skills'.

Zoning allowed a more even distribution of input from both teacher and TA. The less able were not as demanding, and benefited from being able to work more independently. There was less stress for the adults than when dealing exclusively with a group of less able children who are not always willing to cooperate.

The negative elements centred on the difficulties of providing differentiated learning activities successfully. The difference in children's abilities became more obvious in group reading and spelling.

Reflective Teamwork

In Crickwood School, the first teacher-TA pair felt that their relationship was already good before starting the intervention, but attributed an improvement in working practices during the intervention to the fact that their relationship had been strengthened. This, they felt, was due to the structure of Reflective Teamwork 'forcing' them to give each other quality listening time. They also felt that the Reflective Teamwork framework enabled them to problem-solve more effectively, with the result that improvements occurred in the identified group of students within the identified period.

An unexpected finding was that the teacher from Crickwood applied her training and experiences of using this model to her work with students. Following her initial training, she used an increased amount of pairwork with her class, saying that she had been reminded of the value of listening and peer support.

The teacher and assistant from this school felt that this model had empowered the TA to use her insights and knowledge of the children to a greater degree. The teacher gave an example of the TA putting students into pairs in ways that she would never have chosen. The teacher felt that the pairings worked because the TA had more in-depth knowledge of the students' personalities.

At Larch, a widening role for the TA was noticed almost as soon as Reflective Teamwork was used. The teacher noted that within a few days of using this strategy her planning with the assistant was enabling her to be more focused on the needs of individual students. Likewise, the TA found it helpful to be more involved in whole-class planning. Using the model made the teacher think more deeply about planning, and she adapted her teaching following conversations with the TA. The teacher noted that quite often during the paired listening process the TA had said what the teacher wanted to say before she got her turn, showing that their thoughts and responses were more similar than many would expect, given the differential in their training and professional status.

Adaptations to the models

It is worth pointing out that all of the schools developed adaptations of the models in their original forms, and these are noted here.

Room Management (Goldthorpe)

- The idea of 'visiting' was introduced, with a steady circulation from the activity manager. During this, targets could be set and then checked on. This seemed helpful in certain circumstances.
- It was noted that roles must be interpreted flexibly depending on the needs of the students and the nature of the lesson.

- Though the TA seemed to value the extra responsibility, the teacher was dubious about the need or benefit of it. A possible solution lay in stressing the need for the teacher to keep control of 'teacher processes' such as planning, curriculum, enforcement and evaluation.

Room Management (Mableton)

- The model helped to systematize teaching, though there was a good deal of planning required. Ways had to be found of managing this – for example, through negotiating with management for additional, paid planning time.
- There is a need for flexibility. What operated here (very well, *vis-à-vis* the other Room Management group) was what could be called *'intensive groupwork plus light-touch groupwork'* – the one involving a static adult with one group, and the other involving an adult quickly moving from group to group (plus 'visiting').

Zoning (Benfield)

In this school the teacher and TA emerged with some fascinating ideas about the use of Zoning, which could in fact be applied in any of the models. We have summarized their ideas with the mnemonic CHEER, where the C refers to the need to keep extra-demanding groups *central*, the H refers to 'light' or *hovering* support, the first E refers to the need for *experimenting*, the second E refers to the need for the teacher to be the *enforcer*, and the R refers to the need for *roaming* by staff. Thus:

- **Centralizing:** demanding groups are best kept physically **central** to the zone pattern.
- **Hovering:** in an arrangement of groups, where there is differentiation between the amount of support being given – this can be either intensive support or, by contrast, **hover** support.
- **Experimenting:** there is a need for a settling-in period to **experiment** with different zone patterns.
- **Enforcing:** the teacher needs to be the one to maintain structure, direction and discipline for the whole class – to **enforce**.
- **Roaming: roaming** is important, the idea among the children that staff are not static – that they move around a set pattern of tables.

Zoning (Tilsley)

- Zoning promoted mixed-ability work, being best used with differentiation by outcome.

Reflective Teamwork (both schools)

A central benefit of the Reflective Teamwork model was to help equalize relationships between the teachers and the assistants. An effect of this greater parity between the two was that the TAs had increased feelings of empowerment and felt more able to contribute their skills and insights to the planning process. The process appears to have helped break down some of the belief that teachers are the only 'experts' and that the role of the TA is to carry out instructions unthinkingly.

An unanticipated outcome of the implementation of the models more generally is that the teachers and assistants found new definitions and ways of thinking about the notion of special needs, and adopted new ways of working with students designated as having special needs. This followed at least in part from the fact that they were given 'permission' through the research process to use a problem-solving approach.

Comments on Phase 1

The observational analysis and interview feedback both point to substantial improvements being effected in working practice overall, and to differences between the effects of the methods on children's engagement in class. It is worth speculating here on the reasons for the observed effects and differences between methods, given also the corroborative evidence coming from teachers' and assistants' comments.

The implementation of Room Management procedures appeared to produce the most significant increases in engagement. It should be said immediately that the regime of change involved in Room Management is the most radical of all those in the models evaluated here, involving most organizational change with the greatest associated degree of planning, and it is perhaps to be expected that these greater changes would have the most significant effects. It should also be noted that feedback from the participants was most critical about Room Management in terms of the time needed for planning: it was felt that the planning required could not be done without additional time allocation.

Zoning also effected significant changes in both schools where it was tried, though the effects on individual children appeared to be more uneven than those emerging from the Room Management procedures. Zoning constitutes in fact a very simple change in organizational arrangements and it is perhaps to be expected that its effects overall would be less significant than those emerging from Room Management, without the pedagogical planning associated with the latter. However, it is worth noting that the greatest effects engendered from the Zoning procedure appeared to be with those children who had the lowest baseline engagement. This was the case also for Room Management and the implications of this are clear for inclusion: the use of these models appears to systematize the allocation of teacher and TA time and attention to all children and seems to prevent certain children habitually avoiding attention, or certain children becoming saturated with, and over-dependent on, support.

Although the Reflective Teamwork classes showed the lowest differences between baseline and intervention, it should be noted that the mean baseline engagement figures for the students in both of these classes were much higher than those in the Room Management and Zoning classes (83 and 75 per cent, versus 64 to 70 per cent in those other classes). Allied to this, there were no children with very low baseline engagement figures in these classrooms, as there were in the other four. It should be noted also that the Reflective Teamwork participants were the most positive of all the groups in their interview feedback in terms of the benefits that they felt accrued for children. In addition, the Reflective Teamwork model appears to have helped to equalize the power relationships between the teachers and the TAs.

Potential developments following Phase 1 centred on a possible conjoining of these models. Thus one might employ what were taken to be the most effective or meaningful elements of Room Management, Zoning and Reflective Teamwork and use them together in the training of teachers and assistants.

6 Themes from Using the Models in Practice – Phase 1

In this chapter we give more detailed analysis of the verbal feedback of 12 of the teachers and TAs who worked on the three models during Phase 1 of the project. A great deal of interview commentary was collected from these colleagues and this has been organized into *themes* for the purpose of helping to refine understanding of what they were saying to us and to each other about how the models had worked.

The 'master themes' in what follows are the key areas of commonality in respondents' comments; the 'sub-themes' are specific areas of commonality or interest within those master themes. Throughout the presentation of the six main themes, direct quotations from the teachers and TAs directly involved have been liberally included. We hope that these illustrations bring the analysis to life and also suggest avenues for readers' own work in reflecting on, using or adapting the models.

Coding for the schools has been changed for reasons of confidentiality; in this chapter the six schools, all primary, are coded simply A to F. These are represented by the models as shown in Table 6.1.

Table 6.1. The models and the schools

Model	School code
Zoning	A
Zoning	B
Room Management	C
Room Management	D
Reflective Teamwork	E
Reflective Teamwork	F

Master theme 1: there was a change in the role of the TA

This master theme occurred in all of the interview analyses. Each of the three models led to the TA undertaking new and challenging responsibilities. These changes were planned as part of the Zoning and Room Management models and were therefore anticipated. The changes in the TA role encountered in the Reflective Teamwork model were more surprising.

The sub-themes identified within this overall theme of change of role were as follows.

Reduced support for students identified as having special needs and increased support to other students

A key theme identified for all models was a shift for the TA from focusing on a single student or a group of students identified as having special needs to supporting students with different kinds of needs. In the two Zoning schools in particular, TAs took responsibility for a wider range of students. In school A, the TA took on responsibility for a zone comprising two tables of students of all abilities. The teacher commented on how initially the change in focus led the TA to feel concerned about the student she was employed to support.

The TA described feeling: 'that I was being neglectful towards my little boy because I was offering him only hover support and special support if he asked for it'.

In school B, the TA similarly had responsibility for two tables of mixed-ability students. The teacher explained in the following comments how she had changed the focus: 'In the past the TA clearly had a role for supporting kids with special educational needs. Under this system I changed all that ... we all had some special educational needs kids ... She wasn't stuck with the special educational needs table.'

In Room Management school C, the TA took on the role of activity manager with responsibility for keeping four tables of students on-task while the teacher took the table that included the students designated as having special needs. This represented a complete shift in focus from the usual support arrangements where the TA had responsibility for the SEN table.

In Room Management at school D, the TA and teacher shared the activity manager role on alternate weeks. The usual role for this TA was to only take the students identified as having special needs. This change in student focus led to some tensions. The teacher held a strong view that the TA's role was to support the students identified as having special needs and he expressed concern about the TA's ability to work with a broader ability range: 'I was also concerned about the attitudes of the children towards the

TA. The high achievers seemed to like it because they worked well every time R came near but the rest of the time they ignored her.' He also said that the students identified as having special needs were not able to cope without the TA being allocated to deal specifically with them: 'The other thing was, the lowest achievers had to work independently and I don't think they were able to do this. I don't feel that the TA can be activity manager because the children don't respond to her as a teacher. I couldn't expect R to know what to do with the children.'

He found this change in student focus difficult to accept. He seemed to feel that the higher achievers suffered particularly and could also be unsettled and disruptive when supported by the TA. For the TA, the change in student focus led to some real challenges. She was used to supporting a table of students identified as having special needs whom she felt confident of helping: 'When I work with a group I do actually teach them. I feel I can give more input. I really feel I achieve things when I work directly with a group.' Focusing on a broader range of students led to her feeling anxious about the students identified as having special needs whom she did not feel could get on without her help. She said she felt uncomfortable and lacked the confidence to manage the full range of students in the class and that she could not discipline some of the more able students, who ignored her:

> One thing was that when I was activity manager the children played me up whereas when I used to sit with a group under the old system it didn't happen. I felt really embarrassed because if children were getting noisy when I was activity manager, I found it hard to discipline the children because M was in the room. I found the kids were more chatty when I was the activity manager and I didn't feel confident when M was in the room about taking control of the class.

Focus on support to underachieving and demotivated students

In the two Reflective Teamwork schools, it was interesting that both TA and teacher teams chose, independently of each other, to focus on a group of students who were underachieving, rarely completed work, needed frequent refocusing and who could be unsettled and disruptive. Both teachers took the opportunity of the project to focus on what for them represented perhaps the most challenging and unrewarding aspects of their class teaching responsibilities. The teacher at school E explained: 'We focused on students who you normally wouldn't think of as having special educational needs. Kids who don't get their work completed.' Similarly the teacher at school F explained: 'We chose to focus on a particular group of children. We chose underachieving children. We decided that special educaional needs students were getting input already.' And the TA reflected on the shift in focus for her: 'Usually I just work with the special educational needs table. Under this set-up I was working with a completely different group of children and ignoring the special educatioal needs group.'

Prior to the project the TAs had responsibility for groups of students formally identified as having SEN and therefore this represented a major shift in focus. In school E the teacher and TA took joint responsibility for the group and in school F the TA focused on the group alone.

Support to greater numbers of students and more groups

Alongside the type of students supported, there was a change in the numbers of students supported by the TA in the Room Management and Zoning schools. Under Zoning, the zone contained more students than the table which the TA supported previously. The TA at school A noticed that she 'was responsible for more children ... I got to know more children'.

In Room Management, the activity manager had responsibility for larger numbers than the group helper. The teacher at school C commented on how the TA supported more students in total when she undertook this role: 'She had responsibility for a much larger number of children ... she had more students to work with'.

Working with greater numbers of students was not a feature in the two Reflective Teamwork schools, where the TA changed from supporting a group of students identified as having special needs to a small group of around six underachieving students with higher ability.

Noticing individual students and being more aware of their needs

For all three models a theme was identified of TAs getting to know students better so that needs could be more clearly identified. The TA in school A stressed that: 'You, as an adult get to know the children more ... I noticed their strengths and weaknesses more'. Similarly, the TA at school C talked of knowing more students' names as a result of taking on the role of activity manager where she had responsibility for four groups of students. She had previously taken a small group of students designated as having special needs and reflected on how she had only known the names of the students on that table: 'It was amazing, because before doing the model there were definitely a lot of children whose names I didn't know ... I noticed more things about the children and I was able to feed back more to R.'

In the two Reflective Teamwork schools the TAs focused on the targeted group of students to assess their needs more closely and identify what needed to be done to make a difference. The teacher at school F commented: 'She seemed to notice what kind of difficulties they were experiencing ... She got to know the children really well, for example pairing the kids in a way I'd never have thought of.'

Each model was seen to enhance the role of, and increase the demands made on, the TA.

Increased responsibility and increased autonomy

Increased responsibility and autonomy of the TA was a theme regularly noted. For example, in Zoning school A, the TA was now solely responsible for picking up issues on two tables and for making decisions within that zone without referring to the teacher: 'I think she felt her role was heightened, and she was more, if you like, useful. When I looked at her on the video, she seemed to have really become more confident as well. I think it helped her. It reinforced her position in the classroom.'

In Reflective Teamwork school F, the teacher handed over full responsibility for the targeted group of students which led to her increased level of autonomy. The TA commented: 'The opportunity to do my own little project if you like. The focus group was mine.'

Enhanced and widened role

In the Room Management system when the TA undertook the activity manager role, she had complete responsibility for making decisions during the lesson. The teacher at school C commented:

> Her role is much wider because she's the activity manager so she's been responsible for more children, more groups. I was certainly expecting more of her, so she had all these notes and planning notes from me which obviously she had to interpret. The children now see her as someone who works with the whole class and not just with special educational needs students.

Activity manager must manage class and discipline

The increased level of autonomy was extremely challenging for the TA in school D where she took on the role of activity manager on alternate weeks. She said she did not feel confident about managing the class and making decisions and that she felt embarrassed if the students played her up or were noisy. She was worried that being put in this role might lead to a conflict with the teacher. She said:

> When I was activity manager the children played me up whereas when I used to sit with a group under the old system it didn't happen. I felt really embarrassed if children were getting noisy when I was activity manager, I found it hard to discipline the children because 'my' teacher was in the room. I found the kids were

more chatty when I was the activity manager and I didn't feel confident when 'my' teacher was in the room about taking control of the class. As the activity manager I feel I may be treading on 'my' teacher's toes. I don't know if I can manage the whole class.

The very nature of the activity manager role necessitates increased responsibility for the TA and the teacher at school D felt very strongly that TAs should not be asked to take on such extensive responsibility. The difficulties encountered in school D revealed that, for a TA to take on a new role with enhanced responsibility, the teacher and TA need to work closely together and that a great deal of support is required from the teacher. The TA is left in an impossible position if the teacher does not feel positive about the changes.

Change in role of TA: change in status

In all models, the status of the TA was perceived to have been raised.

TA seen as teacher not helper

In Zoning school A, the teacher felt the TA was now regarded differently by the students: 'more of an equal status to the class teacher ... kids sometimes see TA as a helper, but now, they see her much more like a teacher'. This TA had taken on a zone of two tables and undertook a whole range of duties which were at times indistinguishable from those of the teacher.

Students more respectful of TA/students more responsive to TA

In Room Management school C, the teacher noticed students being more respectful of and more responsive to the TA, again a mark of her raised status in the eyes of the students: 'They were very responsive to my TA's support and guidance ... The children were very much more respectful of her help ... I think it did raise her status. The children seemed to really respect her and value her comments and help.'

TA more valued by students and teacher

In both Reflective Teamwork schools the TAs said they felt more valued by the teachers and by the students. The TA in school E said 'I felt I was more valued' and in school F 'P really gave me a free rein and really seemed to value what I was doing'.

One explanation for this was that the guaranteed opportunity to be listened to by the teacher during the 15-minute planning meeting led to the TA feeling that her ideas were highly regarded. One of these TAs described how much better she felt knowing that she would be listened to, in contrast to the previous practice of snatched conversations in the corridor. Joint planning ensured that the TA's ideas and feedback were included in the curriculum planning for the class. The teacher at school E commented on how useful the input was from the TA in the brainstorming sessions: 'I really valued her brainstorming ... The teacher has to realize that the TA has a right to make comments and to value these.' The TA in school F felt valued by being given sole responsibility for supporting the target group of students, describing this group as 'mine'.

Working in these different ways led to the status of the TA being raised, achieved by including them more equally in the planning of lessons, as in the Reflective Teamwork model, by giving them wider responsibilities and by giving them responsibility for a broader range of students to support, beyond dealing with students identified as having special needs.

The changes in the role of the TA led in all three models to the TAs feeling differently about themselves.

TA more confident and happier
In school A the teacher commented on the TA becoming more confident. The TA in turn felt that through Zoning she had made a difference to the lives of the students and really enjoyed the role. She seemed to take on the challenges with enthusiasm. The TA at school C undertaking Room Management was described by the teacher as happier and more confident.

TA embarrassed and lacks confidence
In school D, the TA experienced difficulties because the teacher did not support her to take on the activity manager role. She described herself as embarrassed and lacking in confidence, especially when she was unable to manage the class discipline. She also worried about what the teacher was feeling, knowing that he did not approve of her undertaking the new enhanced responsibilities. Interestingly, even in this school, the teacher thought that the TA had enjoyed aspects of the activity manager role: 'I felt it was unfair to ask her to do it, but I know that R quite enjoyed some of it'.

To summarize, master theme 1 identified a shift from supporting students identified as having special needs to supporting students with a broader range of needs and greater numbers of students. The TA had a more individualized focus on student needs. All models saw TAs with widened roles and increased responsibilities, particularly noticeable for the activity manager role. As TAs took on more challenging work, their status was raised and they were seen differently by all. When things went well, TAs felt more rewarded and happier in these roles, but where not supported they felt undermined and embarrassed.

Master theme 2: effect on teamwork

A second master theme was the effect on teamwork between the teacher and the TA, which occurred in 11 out of 12 interview analyses. Improved teamwork was one of the aims of the study and the effect was positive in five schools and somewhat negative in only one (school D).

The sub-themes identified within this overall theme of effects on teamwork were as follows.

Increased discussion

All three models affected the level of discussion between the teacher and the TA. In Zoning school A, the teacher commented that 'We were doing a lot more chatting together'. The TA at school A gave further detail as to why they needed to talk more: 'We tried lots and lots of different ways of organizing things. So yeah, we did have to work together more as a team. And I was worried about my little boy, so we had more discussions, more experiments.'

Similarly in Zoning school B, the teacher reflected on how the model required more communication: 'I did need to talk to her a bit more about what was going on'. The TA felt that the organization of Zoning required: 'more discussions about the zones'.

The complexities of Room Management necessitated more time to discuss what would be done during a session. The teacher in school C felt she had to provide more support to the TA: 'I've had to give her more planning and perhaps talk to her more'.

Similarly, the TA who undertook the activity manager role found she needed time to discuss it: 'R needed to spend more time explaining things to me'.

Problems finding time to meet

The teacher at school C lamented the lack of adequate time for discussions: 'There was never enough time to discuss with J beforehand what exactly I needed her to do and I tended to rely on giving her written information. I would have liked more time to talk to R.'

The two Reflective Teamwork schools found the daily meetings invaluable yet very difficult to achieve. The teacher at school E noted that: 'The main problem was finding the time, fitting it in', and for the TA this created challenges: 'I was unpaid for the planning time and so I tended to meet at lunchtimes which I needed'. This TA had a son with autism and she needed to use her lunchtimes to complete all the jobs around the house so that she could devote time to him when he returned from school. For the TA in school F finding the time to meet posed similar challenges: 'The most difficult aspect of doing this model is finding the time to do it. Doing the 15 minutes planning meeting was a problem because of D's contracted hours and D kept giving up her time regularly.'

Insufficient time for TA feedback

The issue of feedback was highlighted in one school undertaking Room Management. The TA usually provided support to a small group of students identified as having special needs and then gave feedback on their progress to the teacher. When undertaking the role of activity manager she had responsibility for monitoring 24 students and was unhappy that she could not give feedback on the progress of all these students at the end of a lesson: 'I didn't have time to give feedback to the teacher about 24 students'.

More feedback from TA

By contrast, in the other Room Management school, the model was valued in giving *more* opportunity for feedback. Here, success appeared to be achieved because the teacher made clear her expectations for the amount of feedback.

More time for each other

The Reflective Teamwork class teachers and TAs found that through the daily 15-minute planning meetings they had more time for each other. The TA at school E particularly valued the planning meeting for providing 'the chance to sit down and talk about it as a whole rather than bits of conversations'.

For the TA and teachers trying out new ways of working such as these models, communication proved to be vital. Communication was built in to the model for the two Reflective Teamwork schools and the results demonstrated the value of regular meetings. The other two models necessitated more discussion of how to work together effectively. However, these schools experienced difficulties in finding the time to meet. In school D, the lack of extra meeting time and support led to the TA being unable to perform the activity manager role effectively.

Working together

This 'working together' sub-theme referred to the effect that the models had on teamworking between the TA and teacher. A number of further branches were identified to this sub-theme, as outlined below.

More of a team/no effect on teamwork

One positive outcome for some teachers and TAs was to describe themselves as feeling more of a team. For example, the teacher at school A doing Zoning found that they 'had to work a bit more together and do a bit more teamwork'.

In school D the teacher did not attempt to meet with the TA since she saw it as her role to plan what was to be done and then instruct the TA.

Joint planning

Joint planning was a feature of the Reflective Teamwork schools as a result of the daily planning meeting. The teacher at school E really valued this: 'The big difference was that we were planning together and before we never sat down together ... We were actually meeting and talking which we had just never had time to do.' The TA found it 'helpful to be involved in the planning'. Similarly the teacher at school F commented that 'We planned more as a team and obviously we were meeting every single day'. Again the TA found this was a very different practice to before: 'having a planning structure, 15 minutes a day meant we were planning a lot more often than we used to before'.

Joint planning was not a feature for the Zoning or Room Management schools, although even here the teachers and TAs found that the complexities of the models necessitated more discussion. In these schools the teacher continued to plan alone and to pass on plans to the TA.

Joint training

Joint training and the opportunity to take part in a piece of research together were raised by a number of the participants. For example, the TA at Zoning school B commented that 'It was good that we came out on the training days together'. Similarly the TA at school C doing Room Management school felt that 'It felt quite exciting to be doing a different project together'. The teacher at Reflective Teamwork school F expressed similar views: 'By coming on the training and doing a research project together we saw ourselves more as a team'.

The opportunity to take part in a joint project seemed a rare experience for both TAs and teachers.

Teacher and TA different perspectives

School F doing Reflective Teamwork commented on how the increase in meeting and discussing had revealed the differences in the perspectives of the TA and the teacher. These differences were used effectively when planning for the target group of students. The teacher commented: 'I think the difference between a class teacher and a teaching assistant is our agendas are so different. D says to me get off their case; you're too concerned about their potential, results, SATs. D paired them up in a way I would never have thought of.'

Sharing

The cluster entitled 'sharing the load' referred to the sharing of the challenges and demands of the classroom, which was achieved when the TA and the teacher worked more closely together. What we found interesting in the accounts from which we generated the theme was the level of stress felt by both teachers and TAs as a result of the challenges found in the classroom and how they felt less burdened when they genuinely had another adult to share these with.

Release for the teacher

When the TA and the teacher worked more effectively together, teachers described a sense of release. The teacher at Zoning school A found that he was able to focus effectively on the group of students he was teaching: 'It really released me to get on with teaching one particular group while all the other groups were being catered for'. Exactly the same point was made by a teacher at school C whose TA took the responsibility for four tables of students as activity manager, leaving the teacher to focus on one group.

Even at school D, where the teacher and TA expressed the most negative views about Room Management, the TA noted the benefits for the teacher: 'He could focus entirely on them, because I picked up all the interruptions.'

The teacher in school F described feelings of complete relief and believed this stemmed from the Reflective Teamwork approach which encouraged genuine empathy and support between adults: 'such a relief to be able to share my concerns with another person. I felt an enormous relief, I thought "thank goodness".'

Reduction in adult stress

Linked to this was the idea of a reduction of stress upon the adults. One way this was achieved was through sharing out evenly the demands. The teacher at school A commented on how Zoning forced him to reflect on the mix of students in each zone: 'Questions were arising, for example, about the demands of particular groups and whether you could have two quite demanding groups in one zone.'

And in Reflective Teamwork school F the teacher commented: 'We're sharing students and groups of students more. We're also sharing our experiences. Before I had to be a crab, eyes looking all around.'

Sharing students designated as having special needs

A key feature of sharing the demands related to the sharing of students designated as having special needs. The TA at school A described the distribution of students identified as having special needs: 'Mr H's got a lower ability table and so do I'.

At school B also, doing Zoning, the teacher made a similar comment: 'allocation of children and tables more even, more even in distribution of workload'.

She also commented on the demands of having a table of students identified as having special needs together: 'Because the children were in mixed-ability groups there were only one or two students with very demanding needs in each of the zones. It is terribly stressful if you just have a whole group of less able children who aren't always willing to cooperate and keep demanding. So of course if you mix them up, it's less stressful on the adults.'

The TA at school B commented on the ease of providing support when the students identified as having special needs were more evenly distributed: 'If you've only got one or two children of low abilities in your zone, they get more of your time.'

Role responsibility for zone

An increase in role clarity was raised by both teachers and TAs in the two Zoning schools. The increase in clarity arose from the simplicity of the model so that the TA and teacher knew what they were expected to do and which students to support through having responsibility for a zone in the classroom. The teacher at school A commented: 'Your role was simply to take the complete responsibility for the zone.'

He mentioned the benefits of the system in assimilating additional volunteers into the classroom: 'When we had our parent helper in, I was able to be very clear about what I expected from her, i.e. that was to take a particular group of children in a particular area of the classroom.'

The TA at school A also found the system one of simplicity and clarity: 'You know which geographical zone, which part of the classroom you are responsible for.'

Similarly the teacher at school B commented: [it] made it clearer about who was covering what in that we knew exactly which part of the classroom we were responsible for'. The TA at school B remarked that: 'It was clearer in that I knew which tables I had responsibility for.'

Activity manager role made clear

Room Management similarly increased the level of role clarity, particularly the activity manager role. In school C the teacher noted that: 'J has been clear that she's responsible for the four groups and that she's directly teaching two of them.'

Classteacher gave clearer guidance

In school C the teacher noted: 'She's got a lot more information about my planning and specific teaching points. She is clearer about her role.' Role clarity was not a theme identified in the two Reflective Teamwork schools. For these two schools, themes related more to the quality of the teamwork experience. Issues of role clarity were perhaps less important when significant attention had been paid to developing a good team relationship.

To summarize, master theme 2 was characterized by an increase in the level of teamwork including more discussion between the teacher and TA, although there were pressures in finding the time for this. Joint planning and training, the recognition of the differing perspectives and the unique contribution were themes. Sharing the load of the classroom, including sharing the students identified as having special needs, led to reduced stress. Role clarity increased, particularly for the Zoning and Room Management models.

Master theme 3: improved experience for students

The third master theme was concerned with the effects upon the classroom experience received by the students when the TAs and teachers were more effectively organized as a team. This finding had not been expected at the outset of the research. Although it had been predicted from previous research that more effective deployment of the TA and teacher would lead to students being more on-task, the findings relating to improved general experience were not anticipated. However, the analysis suggested that the teachers and TAs believed there to be important benefits for the students in this regard.

This master theme occurred in all 12 interview analyses. Each model was perceived to have an effect upon the experiences of the students.

More help and praise for students

One clearly articulated view in the Room Management and Zoning schools was that students appeared to get more help. At one level this claim appears unlikely since the models were implemented without additional resources, utilizing the resources already present in the classroom on a regular basis. This was felt to be an important principle because if the findings were to have any practical use for the future then these would have to be for classrooms with a realistic number of staff. Yet it was the perception of the teachers and TAs that more help was available for the students. For example, the teacher at school A said: 'They seem to get more help than before ... they have more access to actual adult help in a classroom.' The teacher in school C doing Room Management similarly felt that more students received help when she commented that: 'more groups of children were receiving support and guidance'. This suggests that when staff are organized more effectively, less time is wasted and students do indeed receive more teaching.

The opportunity to provide extra praise under the Room Management system was noted by the TA at school C: 'I really liked the idea of praising children who were working on-task'. The TA at school D said: 'it did give me a chance to praise the children'.

Students designated as having special needs received more help

The teacher at school A also felt that the students designated as having special needs received more help, despite the fact that they were now included in larger zones and so one would have expected the amount of help available to be less: 'the poorer ones were getting more help'.

No students without help

A related theme in the Zoning and Room Management schools was that no students were left to get on without access to adult support. Under both these models, all students do have an adult allocated to providing them with support. For example, the TA at school B notes that under the Zoning system: 'We didn't need them to be as independent as before, so they didn't feel so isolated and they weren't afraid to ask for help. Because they had a specific person or place to go to.' Similarly in school B the TA commented that: 'Every child has somebody or somewhere they can go ... The children weren't totally independent and didn't feel isolated and they didn't seem worried about asking for help because we'd explained to them that help-wise we were going to provide support for them.'

In Room Management school C the teacher articulated similar views: 'So we didn't expect any groups, even those working independently, just to be able to make a start and get on with it.' And the TA too noted that: 'They always have somebody to go to and we didn't leave any tables to work independently.'

Waiting times reduced/help and praise given more quickly

The waiting times for students to receive help from an adult were perceived to have reduced, and praise and help were given more quickly. The TA at school B commented that the 'waiting time for help was reduced for the children' and she explained her theory as to why this should be: 'The children definitely got attention quicker because there were fewer congregating around one adult and I think we gave them praise and help more quickly and also we could give them the next task.'

Zoning organization explained

In both Zoning schools, the zones were explained to the students so that they knew that help would always be there for them and who to go to. The teacher at school A said: 'I told the children I was looking after two tables and that J was looking after the other three tables.' He explained that the students needed help to understand the Zoning system and who they were to go to for support:

> The students took quite a bit of time to get used to the Zoning system. Right at the first couple of weeks, they just asked whichever adult they wanted, and they completely ignored the zones that we set up for them As time went on, we needed to tell them less about the Zoning and they would go to the person in line with who's zone they were actually in.

The TA made similar comments: 'The children seem to have got an idea of who to go to and if they didn't go to the right place we just needed to give them a gentle reminder.' This was the same in school B, where the TA noticed that: 'We did explain it to the children who were fine about it. Sometimes, I had to remind them.'

Increased individual focus/identifying what makes a difference

Of particular interest was the view that the models led to an increased focus on the needs of individual students rather than groups. The teacher at Zoning school B found she had the chance to really focus on individuals and she liked to work in a child-focused way. She said: 'We could sort of personalize the input and it wasn't focused on a group. So there was much more of an individual focus.' This was most strongly articulated in the Reflective Teamwork schools where the TA and teacher pairs focused on a particular group of students. This gave them the opportunity to focus on these students as individuals, to clarify their needs and to identify what would make a difference.

In school E the teacher noted that the model had enabled greater focus on individuals: 'noticing individual children more rather than groups ... comments are becoming more focused individually and I'm nagging and prodding the children more. I'm just much more aware of the children.' The TA also welcomed this opportunity and commented on how focusing on individuals enabled her to identify what was needed to make a difference: 'We picked up the key issues that make a difference ... You only need to focus individually on the children for about five minutes and you immediately can identify what they need.'

Students listened to more

For Reflective Teamwork school F it was interesting to identify a theme of students being listened to more: 'The training on active listening that we did on the two days really helped us and we used this with the children.' In this school the teacher and TA applied the principles of active listening to the students. They also noticed that students were listening to each *other* more.

Behaviour improved and students more engaged

In Zoning school A, the TA noted that the students' 'behaviour seemed to have improved'. In Zoning school B the teacher noticed that students 'worked more on task and did seem to complete a lot more work'. In school C the teacher noticed a similar improvement: 'children seemed to be on task more'. In school D, although the teacher did not like the Room Management system, she admitted that 'They were on-task more', and this was borne out by the observational analysis.

Improved work habits

The teacher in school F was impressed with the effects of the Reflective Teamwork model: 'The effect on the students was really powerful. After two weeks we felt that the children were beginning to become more motivated, motivated enough to move on.' In school F the TA also noticed an improvement in work habits: 'They seem to be achieving more, doing their work.' And in school C the teacher noticed various improvements: 'There was a lot less distraction.'

Students completed more work

The teacher in school B was pleased that the less able students completed more tasks. Both of the Reflective Teamwork schools noticed an improvement in the work and behaviour of the targeted group of students. In school E the teacher noted 'We noticed improvements; kids who didn't finish their work before now did finish', and similarly the TA noted that 'They were completing their work more'.

More independent work habits/students became more independent

In school C the teacher noticed more independent work habits: 'It seemed to encourage independence ... They got used to working more independently.' The TA in school C expressed similar views: 'we had to encourage the special educational needs students to be more independent because obviously they weren't going to have so much direct intensive help'.

The teacher in school F noted a change in the way the group of students designated as having special needs were responding: 'Obviously the special ecucational needs group weren't getting support by now but they were responding and becoming more independent and becoming more self-motivated.' The last of these comments is particularly important in view of the many comments both inside this project and before it, reported in the research literature, about the possibility of students becoming 'velcroed' to TAs, with all of the attendant dangers of dependence and fatigue.

Students more secure

In Zoning school A, both teacher and the TA said that having the zones explained appeared to make the students feel more secure and happy. The teachers and TAs expressed the view that this was perhaps because students knew who and where to go to if they needed help. The teacher at school A said: 'They knew there would always be help and someone for them'. The TA at school A commented: 'The top students I think felt more secure and their behaviour seems to be better, and the lower tables may feel better because they know they've got TA support. Everybody has got somebody to go to for help, which I think made some feel better.'

To summarize, master theme 3 was about an improved classroom experience for the students when the models were being used. Students were perceived to get more help and praise in Room Management and Zoning. There was an increased focus on the needs of individuals rather than groups. The level of on-task behaviour increased and students developed more independent work habits. Students appeared happier and more secure in the Zoning schools.

Master theme 4: effect of the model on the teacher

This master theme occurred in six interview analyses and thus less consistently over the interviews than do themes 1–3. The sub-themes are presented below.

Effect of the model upon the teacher: increased planning

The teacher had to undertake additional planning in order to implement the models, and this sub-theme occurred consistently in all Room Management and Zoning schools, but not the Reflective Teamwork schools.

The TA at school A undertaking Zoning said: 'I think he had to spend more time planning. He had to tell me a lot more about what two tables were doing whereas before he was just telling me about one.'

At school B, also doing Zoning, the teacher commented: 'I did find the planning more difficult with Zoning.'

Room Management involved the teacher in planning more clearly for the role of the activity manager. For both schools this involved the teacher in planning the activities for the four tables covered by the activity manager, in addition to suitable prompts and worksheets for each table. The teacher at school C worked very hard to make Room Management successful and commented that: 'My planning was more detailed because I put my planning in for J as well … I had a lot more detailed teaching points and notes, prompts for her and ideas about how she might prompt the children and support the children.' Similarly the TA in this school noted that: 'R gave me a whole heap of notes and plans, ideas, particular prompts and so on. Teaching points for each table.'

Increased planning by the teacher was not mentioned in either of the two Reflective Teamwork schools. Here there was an increase in joint planning by the TAs and teachers together – hence the model did not lead to an additional burden for the teacher alone.

To summarize master theme 4, there was increased planning and more support needed for the TA.

Master theme 5: relationship between adult support and student learning

There were generally positive comments about independent learning – referring to the ability of the students to get on alone with their work with minimal help from the teacher. Independent learning skills were referred to in some interviews and were a general aim of the teachers.

Adult support and student dependency

Under Zoning, all students were clear about who and where to go to for help, and indeed this was cited as one of the positives of the system, leading to the students feeling more secure and happier. However, the teacher at Zoning school A was worried that by not leaving the students to get on alone he would not be encouraging them to develop skills of working independently. He said: 'the only concern I had about Zoning was that the students might become dependent on a teacher or the teaching assistant. And that, I really wanted them to develop individual working skills.'

Lowest achievers and independence

Redirecting support away from the students designated as having special needs meant that there was a general concern that this would leave these students to work independently, which they were not used to doing and for which they may lack the skills. The teacher at school D commented: 'The lowest achievers had to work independently and I don't think they were able to do this.' The teacher was keen for *all* students to develop independent working skills, but this was clearly an issue that would require further work. He was also concerned that developing independent learning meant that the students had to be set work that would not challenge them. 'You can't set very challenging tasks, especially for the lower group and I was worried that that would lower the standards.'

Adult support and student learning: differentiation of tasks

Differentiation of tasks was related to supporting students to work independently. The teacher in Room Management school C found that she needed to plan more carefully the tasks that she was providing for the students, particularly when the TA undertook the role of activity manager. Without tasks being at exactly the right level, students required more support than was strictly the role of the activity manager. The activity manager's role was to keep the students on-task by using low-level gestures and prompts, moving quickly from student to student. If the tasks were not differentiated to the right level then this might result in the activity manager spending too much time on one student or group of students and not moving quickly from table to table to keep all students focused. The TA at school C commented that she needed to 'think more about planning to the abilities of the students'.

The teacher at Room Management school D noticed that students were more on-task but attributed this to that fact that they had to be given less challenging work in order to keep them focused while they were being supported by the activity manager. He said: 'The higher achievers are coasting. They are on-task more but that's because we've given them less challenging work.' Much of his concern related to the progress of higher-achieving children: 'I think it's a waste of time because the higher achievers don't achieve as much.'

Adult support and student learning: activity manager role isn't teaching

Themes relating to concern over the role of the activity manager in the Room Management system were raised only by the TA and the teacher at school D. The teacher said: 'I didn't like the role of activity manager who just seemed to be walking around offering prompts. Under the normal arrangements of the Literacy Hour each child gets adult support twice a week. Under Room Management they get adult support once a week so I felt they were getting less support.' The TA felt that the 'activity manager is crowd control, it's not helping them or teaching them'. These comments provided an insight into the beliefs held by teacher and TA about what teaching means and suggested that the supportive role of the activity manager was not explained sufficiently to them or was poorly understood.

Adult support and student learning: support and proximity to students

A significant issue concerned the seating of the teacher and TA in relation to the students' seating. The teacher at Zoning school A felt that one reason for the success of the model was that it enabled the teacher and the TA to be seated in a relatively central position in the zone, resulting in all students being located near to an adult. This enabled the adult to refocus students as they became off-task and it was easier for students to ask for help. The teacher said: 'Now the good thing about this was we could observe the children and give them more hover support and the students didn't go off-task so much. You seem to be able to monitor the students better with Zoning. They seem to work on-task more.'

Refocusing students

The teacher at school E commented on teaching techniques that she and the TA had found to be effective after Reflective Teamwork discussions: 'We targeted them, we kept zooming in, keeping our eye on them, giving them reminders, refocusing them. It was a boost that they needed and I felt it was really successful.'

To summarize master theme 5, adult support and student learning were characterized by sub-themes concerning:

- independent learning improving for all students, but specifically for those identified as having special needs;
- the changing role of the teacher;
- the changing role of the activity manager;
- support and proximity to students;
- the need to plan tasks to match students' abilities.

Master theme 6: special value of Reflective Teamwork techniques

The final master theme was concerned with the special value of specific techniques taught to the Reflective Teamwork pairs and used in the 15-minute planning meeting. This theme occurred in three out of four Reflective Teamwork interview analyses and four sub-themes were identified.

Value of Reflective Teamwork techniques: the evaluation component

The teachers at both schools especially valued the inclusion of an evaluation of the previous lesson in the 15-minute framework. The teacher at school E said: 'It's such a rare thing to evaluate how well things have gone.' The teacher at school F commented on the balance between evaluating what had been done and planning for the future: 'The planning meetings, a very powerful tool; it gives you the chance for really focused discussion about what's gone well and how to move forward. I really like the balance between what you've done well and where we're going.' She had started to use this method with trainee teachers: 'The feedback sheet is a really powerful tool, it allows self-assessment and it shows you the way forward. I'm even using it with the students.'

Value of Reflective Teamwork techniques: the brainstorming component

Both teachers valued brainstorming. The teacher at school E valued the opportunity to brainstorm for the next session and noted how much more productive this was with another adult. She regarded her TA as having some particularly useful ideas which they were able to work up together: 'It was the brainstorming together that made the difference.' Similarly, the teacher at school F met with the TA and brainstormed different ways of moving the target students on, and really valued this experience.

Value of Reflective Teamwork techniques: the active listening component

The TA at school F regarded active listening as a very powerful tool: 'Active listening is ingrained in everything I do.'

To summarize, master theme 6 was concerned with the value of techniques taught to the Reflective Teamwork pairs – specifically evaluation, brainstorming and active listening. Striking was the use of the word 'powerful' in these transcripts.

7 Action Research into the Models – Phase 2: 'Working Together'
with Carol Connell

Working together – the development of new models

A year after Phase 1, the models of Room Management, Zoning and Reflective Teamwork had been evaluated and there was the opportunity to consider how the models might be developed or conjoined – or both.

Thus in Phase 2, the six new schools with whom we were working were given a far freer rein about the ways that they would work with their classes. A training day was again provided detailing the models and the ways in which they had been used in Phase 1, but colleagues were now asked to select from the models the elements that would suit the needs of their settings. There would thus be a 'mix-and-match' of the models, taking the most useful elements of each depending on local circumstances and preferences.

Furthermore, a more user-centred approach was taken to data collection and analysis. While in Phase 1 detailed researcher-directed methods were used (with videotapes made of classrooms and a research assistant assessing engagement figures), in this second phase colleagues were asked to make their own recordings of classroom activity in a simplified way. Feedback on the methods was similarly problem-centred, using interviews as in Phase 1, but also using more collegial, large-group gatherings which acted as problem-solving sessions as well as evaluations.

Throughout this phase there was thus a developmental and action research thrust that was not wholly characteristic of Phase 1. Feedback from teachers and TAs was more open-ended and informal, and the reporting of this feedback reflects this informality. Likewise, the collection of engagement data, which was undertaken by staff in their own settings, with restricted time and facilities for analysis, sometimes relied on more limited data than was available in Phase 1.

The new project, Phase 2, was named '*Working Together*'. As previously noted, the schools in this phase comprised both secondary and primary. The three secondary schools we have named Jewell, Cooke and Calthorpe. and the three primary schools we named Oscarson, Lightmead and Parkway.

Please note that in our report of findings in this chapter and subsequently, there is reference in our respondents' comments to LSAs. There is some confusion nationally over nomenclature for TAs – in some LEAs, the term 'LSA' refers to all kinds of TA, whereas in others it refers to just those with specific responsibilities for children designated as having special educational needs. In our own text we use 'TA' to apply to all types of assistant.

Practice pre-intervention

Numbers of TAs were quite similar (averaging nine) in each school, regardless of school size and sector. The titles and profiles of TAs, and the ways in which they were deployed, however, differed between schools, even within sectors. In Lightmead, for example, TAs were paid for attending a staff meeting once a fortnight, which included 30–40 minutes of team planning time, whereas in Parkway, an infant school, the role of the TA was much wider and included sitting with students in assembly and preparing displays. The differences were particularly marked between the primary and secondary sector. In general, primary school TAs were attached to classes, whereas secondary school TAs were attached to individual students, particularly those with statements of SEN or at School Action Plus (SA+) of the SEN *Code of Practice*.

Some attempt was made in two of the three secondary schools to link TAs to particular faculties or departments so that they could work to their strengths and build up a working relationship with particular colleagues, but the focus generally remained on supporting particular students. This was also evident in the more frequent practice at secondary level of withdrawing students for one-to-one or small-group support with a TA, usually managed by a SENCO or senior TA.

Key issues pre-intervention

What then were the key issues that the schools were hoping to address though collaborating with this research? In general these can be summarized as:

- Improving teaching and learning in inclusive settings.
- Improving planning for teacher-TA teams through making time for discussion and collaboration.
- Raising the profile of TAs.

Key issues pre-intervention for secondary schools

A general problem that all secondary project teachers and TAs highlighted was that TAs often found themselves having to adopt a range of roles according to the needs and the style of individual teachers. This leads to variable practice, and the tendency for TAs to take on a reactive rather than a proactive role.

The project teacher and TA at Jewell identified the need to focus on the role of the TA in order to improve teaching and learning for inclusion, and in order to improve communication between TAs, teachers and senior managers. This was echoed at Cooke, where the project teacher wanted time to think and plan for the effective use of TAs. Linked to this (although beyond her remit in school, and beyond the scope of this research) she noted also that she would have liked to have been in a position to provide opportunities for performance management, and enhanced career progression for TAs.

The project teacher and TA at Calthorpe were perhaps the least satisfied with existing practice. They both referred to it as 'mixed', with some students being given 'Velcro support' with a TA constantly at their side. The project teacher noted that 'many teachers do not plan, and are very offhand in the way they treat LSAs'. The TA went further by saying that some teachers treated TAs 'quite badly' and that there was a lack of courtesy on the part of teachers, some of whom did little to collaborate with TAs other than expecting them to deal with the problem behaviours of 'their' students.

Key issues pre-intervention for primary schools

At primary level, the key issues were not dissimilar to those of secondary colleagues. The project teacher and TA at Oscarson acknowledged that teachers and TAs in their school did plan together, but that this was done 'on the hoof' without any particular structure. This sometimes resulted in TAs not having proper access to plans for individual sessions, and not having opportunities to feed into the planning process early enough to have an impact. Not only did they feel that this affected the profile of the TA, who in these situations is less able to make a significant contribution to the lesson, but it also affected the way in which the TA was able to work with individual students, sometimes causing TAs to focus too much one student, rather than providing 'hover support' which might enable students with special needs to interact more with their peers.

The project teacher and TA at Lightmead linked the need for more time for discussion, planning and collaboration with a need to ensure greater consistency across classrooms. At Parkway, the link was made between enhanced teacher-TA communication, raised standards through 'smarter working' and the opportunity for 'everyone to develop their potential in a happy environment'. Thus this project was seen as a means of capacity-building among both children and adults.

The implementation of Working Together procedures in the six schools

As each school implemented Working Together procedures slightly differently, information about how the project was translated into each school context is given below. (As a reminder, the three secondary schools are Jewell, Cooke and Calthorpe and the three primary schools are Oscarson, Lightmead and Parkway.)

Jewell (secondary)
In this school two classes were identified to take part in the project, one Year 11 class working with an experienced teacher, whose students were described by the project teacher as demotivated, and one Year 8 mixed-ability class who were working with an unqualified teacher. In this school the chosen model was Zoning. Problems of finding time for Reflective Teamwork and planning were highlighted in this school.

Calthorpe (secondary)
In this school the implementation of the project was hampered by illness among key staff. This raises the issue of a lack of cover for TAs in schools. The classes chosen for the project were hand-picked due to the fact that the project teacher and TA felt that they would be sympathetic to the aims and values of Working Together procedures. Thus, two 'bottom set' English classes were chosen, one Year 8 and one Year 9. A high proportion of students in these classes were described by the project teacher and TA as having special needs and behavioural difficulties. They were also felt to have poor group-work skills. The teacher and TA chose either Room Management or Zoning depending on the groupwork tasks being undertaken.

Cooke (secondary)
At Cooke, four classes were chosen, three of them (mixed-ability English, science and geography) from Year 7, and one all-female textile group from Year 10. Either Room Management or Zoning were chosen according to groupwork tasks set, and teachers and TAs from each class involved in the project aimed to meet for a total of 15 minutes per week. This was not always possible due to competing commitments, and some teachers and TAs varied the amount of time spent – for example, two one-hour meetings instead of regular slots. Sometimes planning took place at the beginning or end of lessons, during break-times or in snatched conversations before or after school. Finding the time for this planning was identified as the biggest problem for the effective implementation of Working Together procedures.

Oscarson (primary)
The teacher at Oscarson described her infant school's structure as 'complex', with mixed year groups and many TAs doing a few hours each. Nevertheless, she wanted Working Together procedures to be implemented

in every classroom in the school. Her action plan was therefore carefully constructed in order to ensure effective communication between all parties.

She began the process of implementation by briefing the senior management team on the aims and scope of the project, and this was followed by a (remunerated) in-service training day for all staff led by herself and the project TA. The project teacher describes how she set out the chairs for the day in small groups of three and asked each class to sit in 'their team' – something that had never been done before. Taking her lead from the researchers, who had been keen to impart ownership on the project teachers and TAs, she pointed out that 'they could find their own way of working together and we wanted them to do what they felt comfortable with'. Each teacher and TA was given an information pack, which included customized handouts, adapted from original course materials. Several of the listening and teamwork activities that the project teacher and TA had experienced as part of their own training featured in the training that they provided for their colleagues. This had the result that 'everyone was amazed at how much they learnt about each other in such a short time', and 'the research went well, all the staff were interested in being involved in the research'.

It was decided that there would be a weekly slot for teachers and TAs to engage in Reflective Teamwork and planning during whole-school assembly. The most frequently used model was Zoning, which was used for most subjects (including art, science and PE) with Room Management being used just for information technology and literacy. Where Room Management was used, the activity manager was nearly always the teacher. Three classes used Room Management to enable the teacher or a TA to do daily early reading research (ERR) sessions with individual children. According to the project teacher, this had 'a big impact on their word recognition skills'. The project was highly motivating for all staff in the school, with many lively discussions and friendly rivalry about which class was the most on-task.

Lightmead (primary)

In this junior school all classes in the school participated in the project. It was presented to all teachers and TAs during a meeting that took place as part of the school's informal half-termly meeting programme. Each teacher and TA was given a pack of materials. Time for Reflective Teamwork and planning was made by the headteacher taking the whole school for assembly twice a week for 20 minutes. The process of gathering data generated a lot of discussion between teachers and TAs, and the findings were felt to have relevance beyond this research. Both Zoning and Room Management were used in this school, as shown in Table 7.1:

Table 7.1. Zoning and Room Management at Lightmead

Class/Year	Lesson	Model
3G	Numeracy	Zoning
3G	Literacy	Room Management
3T	Numeracy	Zoning
4H	English	Room Management
4H	Maths	Zoning
4R	Maths	Zoning
5M	Numeracy	Zoning
5L	Numeracy	Room Management
6C	Numeracy	Zoning
6W	Numeracy	Zoning
6W	Literacy	Room Management

It can be noted that, in general, the estimation was that Zoning would be more useful for numeracy, whereas Room Management would be more useful for literacy. This echoes the findings from Oscarson.

Parkway (primary)

In this infant school both Room Management and Zoning were used in several classes for numeracy, although data from only nine students were collected. A carefully managed process was used to introduce the models to teachers and TAs. First the models were trialled by the project teacher and TA in their own classroom, and some amendments were made. Following this, two in-service training sessions were provided for all staff by the project teacher and TA. The project teacher then made further opportunities available for TAs to observe Room Management in action in her class. The effective implementation of these models was made a performance management target for the TAs.

This school was already using initiatives such as 'brain gym' and 'feelings trees' at the start of each day to improve children's concentration. During the trial period, the project teacher and TA decided to introduce a ten-minute period of game-playing just prior to the groupwork section of the Numeracy Hour (in which Room Management techniques were to be used) in order to improve further the children's ability to remain on task. Reflective Teamwork and time for planning was made available by paying the TAs to come into school early, at 8.45 a.m., for a meeting with their teacher. Teachers felt challenged to produce clearer plans that could be understood by TAs, and an 'open book' system was introduced for teachers and TAs to capture comments that could not be made face to face immediately.

Evaluations of Working Together procedures from the schools

Jewell (secondary)

In the Year 11 class, Zoning was used to support the TA to work closely with a target group of students. This improved the on-task behaviour of all students considerably. The project teacher was interested to note that the process of data collection through observation revealed that those students who were on-task were not those that the teacher would have predicted. The use of the TA to motivate and support particular students was, however, dependent on the availability of the TA, and the teacher commented that unless these students continued to be targeted they remained demotivated.

In the Year 8 class, Zoning also improved the on-task behaviour of all students. The project teacher and TA felt that this was because the class knew that the TA and teacher were working together as a team. As the teacher was new to the school and inexperienced, Zoning with an experienced TA helped her to establish herself. The project teacher was concerned about the fact that such a high level of adult supervision appeared to be necessary to keep students on-task during individual and groupwork.

The engagement figures recorded by staff at Jewell for Years 8 and 11 are shown in Figures 7.1 and 7.2.

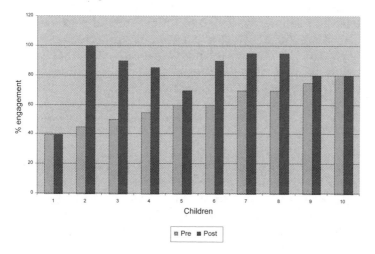

Figure 7.1 Engagement figures at Jewell, Year 8

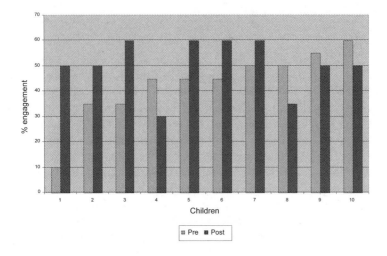

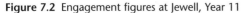

Figure 7.2 Engagement figures at Jewell, Year 11

Calthorpe (secondary)

In this school, where the project was hampered by illness among key staff, little progress was made. The project teacher and TA did note, however, that where they had been able to use Reflective Teamwork and plan together, this was particularly useful. They felt that 15 minutes of focused planning time was enough. The key issue for them was that each TA in their school was working with up to 15 teachers, thus making this level of teamwork and planning difficult to implement. They also felt that student attitudes towards the role of the TA would also need to be challenged if progress were to be made.

Cooke (secondary)

The project teacher at Cooke provided comprehensive documentary evidence of a thorough and well-researched project in her school. In addition to the data required by the researchers, she interviewed all teachers and TAs involved in the project in order to gain deeper insights into how Working Together procedures were implemented in practice and how they were evaluated by teachers and TAs.

In general, both teachers and TAs at Cooke recognized Room Management and Zoning as existing practice. The main element that they felt was new was the Reflective Teamwork and planning aspect of Working Together procedures. In their descriptions and evaluations of Zoning and Room Management, however, it became clear that some of the procedures involved in these models were not existing practice. A TA using Room Management in a Year 7 geography lesson noted that she made sure that she supported a range of students with a task set if the teacher was the learning manager with 'her' target student. She felt that the all students seemed pleased to accept her help. Another TA, using Zoning in a Year 7 English lesson, commented that the teacher she was working with was slightly less comfortable than she was with her changed role. This teacher was a little concerned if the TA worked with other students and left a child with relatively severe learning difficulties to work on his or her own for more than a few minutes. The TA, however, saw this as a natural role for herself, and had been trying to work in this way for some time in order to promote the independence of her target students. She felt that although the teacher was reluctant to use Zoning, in the event it was very successful. Students who in the past had thought that she was there for particular students responded very well: 'which stood us in good stead when the teacher was absent and another member of staff covered the lesson. All of them were happy to approach me for help with the task set.' Thus she is suggesting that an enhanced role for TAs can help to provide continuity in situations where there is a degree of staff absence or staff turnover.

This TA would have liked to have had more access to detailed lesson planning in order to maximize her effectiveness. She would have found it useful to have had a note of key points that the teacher wanted to cover (more detail than lesson objectives) and more information about what the teacher wanted the students to achieve. She would have found this more useful than joint planning time. The other three TAs and teachers, however, found the Reflective Teamwork and joint planning element of Working Together procedures extremely useful. The TAs felt that it engendered a positive approach which meant that they were 'able to sort out any problems as and when they arose'. The teachers listened well, encouraged their comments, were supportive of their ideas and appreciated their input. One of the teachers commented that she would like to be given time to plan and work more closely with the TA on an ongoing basis, as she valued opportunities for joint planning, sharing objectives and assessing situations together. According to the teachers, the TAs gave their comments confidently and constructively and made valuable observations that the teachers had not considered. Time, not the need for training, was identified as the main impediment to this way of working.

The engagement figures for Cooke are shown in Figures 7.3 and 7.4.

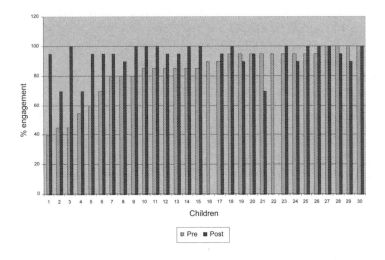

Figure 7.3 Engagement figures at Cooke, Year 7

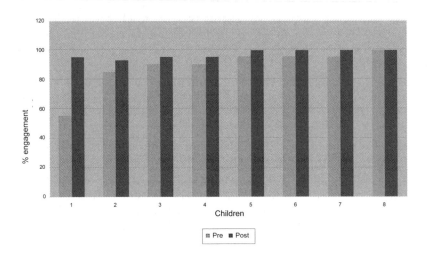

Figure 7.4 Engagement figures at Cooke, Year 10

Oscarson (primary)

The project teacher at Oscarson reported on the findings from her school in terms of positives for teachers, TAs and children, and negatives in more general terms. She based this on her own perceptions and the findings of a post-intervention questionnaire that she designed for every teacher and TA in the school. There were many positives for teachers. From the point of view of classroom organization, they were more aware of different methods and more inclined to vary the way they organized their class. Teachers were

more able to teach effectively by dividing up the class to suit the requirements of the lesson. They were less likely to expect the TA to work with
small groups or individual students, and felt less guilty about working with
smaller groups themselves. Teachers had been freed from some administrative tasks due to greater delegation to TAs. The project teacher felt that there
was more flexibility of thought about many things, since deep-rooted ways
of thinking had been challenged, for example, 'the balance of power in the
classroom'. Increased teamwork was evidenced through 'more dialogue'
and teachers feeling 'more supported working as part of a class team, and
more able to admit to failure or difficulty'. Behaviour issues 'were easier to
solve with a team approach and time to discuss them'.

The TAs 'felt more valued as a group' with 'a new respect shown to
them'. New skills had been discovered and were beginning to be used. They
enjoyed working as part of a closer team with opportunities to effect change
in their classrooms, through a more imaginative use of their time. They
liked the increased clarity that being given specific responsibilities gave
them, and they liked working with a greater variety of children, including
the most able. More school and class information was being shared with
them, such as medium and weekly plans, and performance and assessment
report details. Their views were being sought on a variety of issues such as
how to manage the children at lunchtime, or what they thought about the
new reading method (ERR). The TAs enjoyed having a more equal part to
play in class, and liked the fact that the project assumed they really did
have a big impact on the children's progress. They also liked the increased
status afforded them by children and parents. They had started to express
themselves more openly in the staff room, where they were: 'much more
noticeable and vociferous'. There had been 'a big increase in general discussion, involving TAs, about teaching and learning, job descriptions of
TAs, TA responsibilities in school, etc.'. Previously TAs had 'not been
involved in this'.

Students benefited from knowing whom they needed to go to. They
'have become used to working with a wider range of adults'. They have
'seen a more equitable division of labour within the school staff', and 'have
enjoyed having their views canvassed' (through the student questionnaires). According to the project teacher, the project TA and the class teachers, they also benefited from better organized classrooms and better class
behaviour management.

There were also some negative outcomes from Working Together procedures. A great deal of time was needed to set up the project, collect the
data and write up the findings. One teacher felt that 'the TAs were being
exploited, as they were not paid to take on such responsibilities' and some
TAs felt that 'other TAs might not want to take on extra responsibilities, particularly the older ones'. Some TAs did not feel that the teachers were genuinely devolving their power: 'some teachers paid lip-service to the idea of

teamwork, but in reality they continued to have all the power'. From a practical point of view, teachers disagreed about the frequency of the weekly meetings, with some wanting them less frequently and others wanting them daily. Money was highlighted as an issue, as TAs had been funded to participate in these weekly meetings for the period of research. There was no guarantee that these funds would be ongoing.

Engagement figures recorded by staff for the different years in which the project ran at Oscarson are shown in Figures 7.5 to 7.7

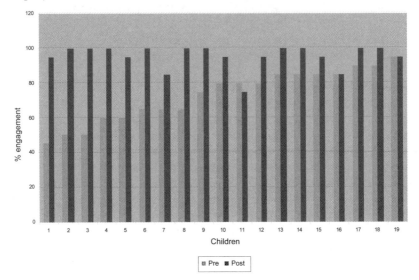

Figure 7.5 Engagement figures at Oscarson, Year 6

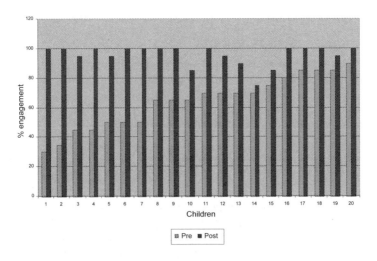

Figure 7.6 Engagement figures at Oscarson, Year 5

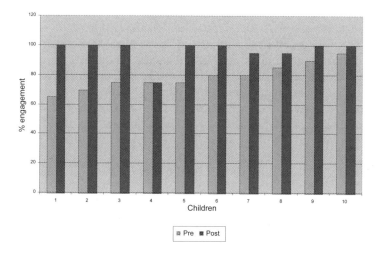

Figure 7.7 Engagement figures at Oscarson, Year 4

Lightmead (primary)

The Year 3 teachers and TAs in this school particularly valued Reflective Teamwork, as it 'got us talking', and made them 'mutually aware of issues'. This led to a team approach to planning and implementing change. They appreciated being given a structure for Reflective Teamwork which enhanced the quality of their listening. One grateful Year 3 teacher reflected: 'What would I do without my TA?' Zoning and Room Management had the benefit that children were calmer and more controlled, and generally produced a higher quality of work, partly because they knew who to go to for help, and partly because there were increased opportunities for one-to-one support. Children tended 'not to follow adults around so much' with all children in the class receiving some adult attention at some point. The negatives of Zoning and Room Management in Year 3 tended to centre on issues of disparity, with not all ability groupings receiving equal amounts of help. Lower achievers 'seemed to need constant attention', which is not always possible using these models.

The findings from Year 4 were not so positive. One Year 4 teacher noted that, with Room Management, 'We find that when we are the "activity manager" we spend most of our time explaining and going over things with individuals. The children have become dependent on us and seem not to be able to get on with work on their own.' Previously 'we were both activity managers, specifically targeting a group each day, and we expected the rest of the class to get on independently, which they did!' This resulted in the teacher and TA: 'reducing our teaching by half'. With Zoning: 'children appear to be off-task more, and we often seem to be flitting here there and everywhere. We feel more like helpers than teachers!' The only 'positive' was that they could 'go round marking, so less of our own time is wasted marking books. However, does this really benefit the children?'

The Year 5 teachers and TAs also raised the issues of independent learning, although they were more positive in general about the benefits of Working Together procedures. They felt that the children benefited from a more focused approach, with key adults getting to know them better and planning more effectively for their learning. They noted that 'the children are more confident, gaining mathematical skills, and are not afraid to ask, so that we can intervene with problems sooner'. From the point of view of teamwork, they felt that there were 'clearer expectations for both the teacher and the TA', and that it was: 'great to have time to communicate effectively'.

The Year 6 teachers and TAs valued the fact that Zoning 'enables the class teacher and TA to focus on specific groups of children, targeting key skills without being interrupted'. In this way 'the weaknesses/strengths/learning styles of individual students are easier to identify and cater for'. As with some of their colleagues, they felt that one of the main benefits of these models was greater role clarity, and that one of the main challenges was managing the 'lower ability zone', which could become 'very busy and demanding'. Unlike some of their colleagues, they saw it as a positive that they were more able to carry out marking and assessment with greater success. In Room Management, they liked the fact that the profile of the TA was raised with the children, but they did not like the fact that the teacher had less input into small-group teaching when she or he was an activity manager rather than an individual/group helper. The Year 6 teams particularly benefited from Reflective Teamwork, which they saw as 'invaluable'. Some of the main benefits were for the TAs who 'gained greater insight into [the] thinking behind planning' and were able to contribute more to the planning process. This led to 'greater feelings of teamwork'.

Engagement figures recorded by staff for the different years in which the project ran at Lightmead are shown in Figures 7.8 to 7.11.

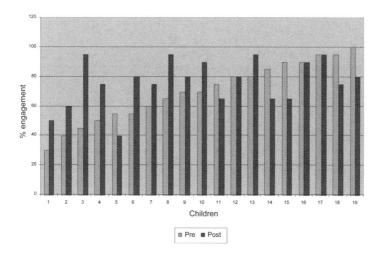

Figure 7.8 Engagement figures at Lightmead, Year 6

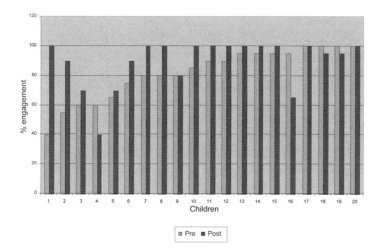

Figure 7.9 Engagement figures at Lightmead, Year 5

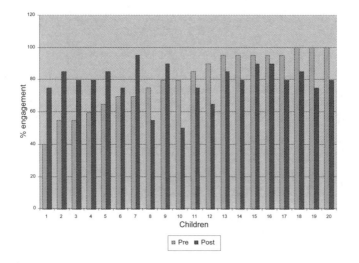

Figure 7.10 Engagement figures at Lightmead, Year 4

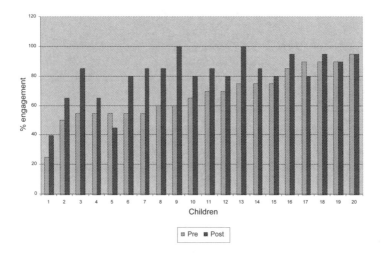

Figure 7.11 Engagement figures at Lightmead, Year 3

Parkway (primary)

At Parkway, an infant school, Working Together procedures were positively evaluated by the project teacher and TA. This was largely due to increased opportunities for effective communication. The TAs were given higher-quality information concerning not only the learning objectives for each session, but also the reasoning behind the plans. This resulted in greater flexibility and in the coverage of more activities with the children. The TAs have also felt more able to communicate their knowledge of the children to the teachers, and to attend staff meetings. The one negative highlighted was that a third person can 'throw the equation'. Ongoing issues were to ensure that 'TAs and teachers continue to make real time for Reflective Teamwork' as 'It is easy to think you are doing this when in reality you are only paying it lip-service'.

The engagement figures recorded by staff are shown in Figure 7.12.

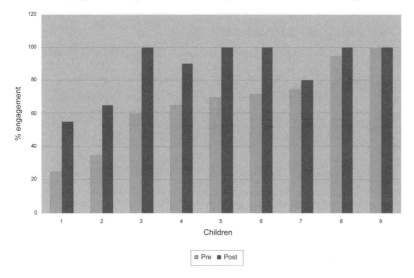

Figure 7.12 Engagement figures at Parkway School

A case study in one secondary school

In the following, Carol Connell, one of the teachers involved in the project, describes how she used the ideas from Working Together and developed them into her own adaptation: a system of 'Working Together slips' and a method that she labelled '360↻'. She describes a highly successful development that evaluation proved to be valuable in enabling communication between team members and in facilitating planning and pedagogy.

Carol Connell, school-based project leader, Cooke school

The Cooke Community School joined the research project in 2002/3. There were two developments that arose from the project based in the school:

•   the Working Together slips
•   the 360↻

Working Together slips for Reflective Teamwork

Finding time for TAs and teachers to reflect and plan collaboratively is without doubt a significant challenge. As an aid to the process of reflecting and planning, an A5-size Working Together slip was devised to enable and maintain Reflective Teamwork and the increased communication between teacher and TA (see below).

LSAs/Teachers Working Together Slip		
To _____ Teacher/TA	**From** _____ Teacher/TA	**Date** _____
Subject	A&D/De/D&T/Dr/En/Fr/Ge/H/ICT/Ma/Mu/Pa/PE/RE/Sc	
Date	_____ *Day* M/Tu/W/Th/F *Period* 1/2/3/4/5	
Lesson Activity	•	
Learning objective	•	
RM/ Zoning/ 360°↻ Details		

The 360↻

The 360↻ came about from observing TAs and teachers working together in the classroom, together with discussions about ways of working in the classroom with my assistant learning support coordinator and senior LSA, Margaret Stone, who was the lead LSA for the project in the school. In a nutshell, the 360↻ is a combination of circulation and hover support where members of staff in the classroom aim to circulate and support without being in the same area at the same time.

For evaluation of these innovations, questionnaires were issued to all teachers and TAs before implementation of all the Working Together models including the 360↻ and Working Together slips, and at the end of the spring term 2004 during the twelfth week of implementing the Working Together approach. In order to be more manageable, staff were asked to focus upon using the Working Together slips for students with statements of SEN in Key Stage 3.

Analysis of questionnaires

It was decided to focus on TA feedback as a more comparable number of responses for both pre- and post-interventions were received from TAs. There were closed and open questions in both questionnaires which gave the TAs the opportunity for personal reflection and the chance to gain more insight into how the work was developing.

In the pre-intervention questionnaires, just under half of the TAs (45 per cent) felt that they did not have planning time with the teacher. Analysis of the TAs' descriptions of their work in classrooms identified four key areas which could be used for training purposes:

1   The TA's *modus operandi*.
2   Keeping students on-task generally.
3   Specific interventions for students' needs.
4   Communication with teacher.

Analysis of the post-intervention questionnaires indicated that nearly all TAs (92 per cent) felt that they had more lesson/planning information from the teacher and that communication between the teacher and themselves had increased. Half of the TAs also felt that the teacher worked with 'learning support' students more.

TAs were also asked to place in order of preference the different Working Together approaches that they would continue to use or encourage other TAs and teachers to use. The 360⟲ model had the highest ranking followed by Zoning, Working Together slips and finally Room Management.

According to the TA responses, there was a doubling in the lesson planning information from the teacher to the TA. This development in itself seems to demonstrate that by describing methods of Working Together and by having an expectation from the TA and teacher that such Working Together methods will be used, the communication between TA and teacher increases.

It is also clear from the TAs responses that the lesson planning information from teachers was valued. They appear to feel more effective by having this knowledge. It also appears that by giving TAs the language to describe their working practices, they are able to communicate with the teacher more, and *vice versa*. In particular, Reflective Teamwork certainly seems to engender a two-way process.

Conclusions

It seems to be that by giving TAs and teachers methods of working together and a 'language' for working together, teamwork and the awareness of its impact on student engagement is strengthened. Furthermore, TA confidence has risen. As one TA said: 'Students are more cooperative with me in lessons when they see the teacher talking to me.' This TA clearly feels that this communication gave her status in front of the students and that she was identified as being part of the 'teaching team'. In those lessons, she was able to be more effective as a result of what the students saw happening between herself and the teacher.

Since September 2004, the Working Together slips have been used throughout the school rather than just being focused in Key Stage 3, and the 360↻ is now embedded as a Working Together approach alongside Room Management, Zoning and Reflective Teamwork (including the Working Together slips).

A personal note

I can certainly say that being involved in this teacher-practitioner research has been one of the most exciting, interesting and informative projects I have ever worked on. The interventions when implemented have had an impact. I've seen TA confidence improve, teachers using TAs more effectively and students' engagement rise.

Summary of findings about the models

The following represents a summary of feedback from teachers and TAs about the various models that they trialled in different ways over the whole period of the research.

Room Management

Positives

- Most TAs enjoyed a new extended role.
- Learning managers were able to work with target groups of students without as many interruptions.
- Overall, more students were receiving support and guidance.
- There was increased respect for TAs in staff and classrooms, and from parents.
- Students identified as having special needs were less dependent on the TA with resulting increases in self-esteem.
- Teachers were more able to work with the full ability range.
- Teachers were less likely to expect the TA to work with individual students, and felt less guilty about working with individuals themselves.

Negatives/issues
- Some TAs were not confident managing the main body of the class.
- Some teachers were concerned that it is not fair to expect a TA to take responsibility for managing the activities of the whole class.
- Increased planning time is needed.
- Some groups of students did not have adequate skills for autonomous learning when neither teacher nor TA was immediately available.

Zoning

Positives
- Most TAs felt empowered by Zoning and more effective as a result.
- Teachers found it easier to monitor students' work and behaviour.
- Teachers were more able to get on with teaching one small group.
- Fewer students were moving around the room and queuing.
- Less able students received more help from the teacher, and were not seen as a separate group.
- Zoning was useful when extra people (parent helpers) came into the class.
- Zoning enabled more mixed-ability teaching.
- Students got attention more quickly.
- Most students developed increased autonomy and peer support skills.
- There was a more even distribution of teacher and TA support across the class.
- There was improved role clarity for teacher and TA.
- Zoning was useful for subjects such as design technology, science, and art.

Negatives/issues
- It takes time for stable patterns of group configurations to emerge.
- Some students became more dependent on adult input as a result of increased adult attention.
- If lower-ability students are grouped together, this zone can be demanding for one adult and problems of 'ghettoizing' students emerge.

Reflective Teamwork

Positives

- It created generally improved communication and working practices.
- Although mostly already strong, the teacher-TA relationships were improved through the team participants being 'forced' to give each other quality listening time.
- There was more effective problem-solving.
- There were improvements in learning.
- The TAs felt empowered to use their insights and knowledge of the students to a greater degree.
- There was a widened role for TAs.
- There was reduced stress, and benefits of feeling listened to.
- Teachers adapted planning and were more reflective following the 15-minute planning meetings.
- It provided a good vehicle for discussing students at risk, and for improving behaviour.
- There was no loss of face in discussing problems. This was due to the small team size and atmosphere of trust established by the listening framework.
- TAs were more able to offer continuity when supply teachers were in, due to increased knowledge of planning.
- Teachers and TAs were more aware of different models for organizing the class, and more inclined to experiment and divide up the class to suit the requirements of the lesson.
- More school and class information, such as medium and weekly plans, were shared with TAs.
- TAs' views were increasingly sought on a variety of issues, such as how to manage the children at lunchtime, or what they thought about the new reading method.

Negatives/issues

- Lack of time for planning.
- Some TAs had to use their free time to participate in planning, and if paid time was not provided by the school the system was therefore unsustainable.
- It was difficult to implement where TAs work with many different teachers, especially at secondary level.

PART 2
Implementation in Schools

Introduction

We expect that the first part of this book will have given the reader some idea of:

- the changing role of the TA today – a broader role in which there is far more involvement in the learning of the child;
- the challenges that TAs and teachers face in working together and the need to implement practices that will enable effective teamwork;
- the kinds of activities – in pedagogy and behaviour management – in which TAs will be working with teachers, and ways of helping children's learning through TAs and teachers engaging in reflective practice;
- different potential models of working and the findings of our research in which we evaluated these models by looking at the effects the models' implementation, and by asking teachers and TAs how they felt about using the models.

We hope that readers will have been able to read enough of this material to make an assessment of the kind of innovation they would like to experiment with in their own classrooms or schools.

The material in Part 2 focuses on the practical business of making a change of this kind – a change to a more professional, organized type of teamworking between teacher and TA.

Throughout, the assumption is that there are no hard and fast answers when it comes to introducing a change in the classroom, and that such change has to be researched as it is introduced, and evaluated in practice. Thus, while we give – for guidance – outlines for the different models that we trialled, we give as much prominence in this part of the book to ways of assessing the effects of any change that may be introduced. These suggestions for undertaking action research are given in Chapter 10.

We have also provided some ideas on activities for CPD. Such CPD might be just for one class, or for several in a school or group of schools.

All materials are photocopiable for use within one school, though we ask that permission is sought from the publishers for wider duplication. Selected parts of the materials are also downloadable in A4 format from www.openup.co.uk/vincett

8 Using the Models

Room Management

Room Management is a system for helping the staff within a classroom to work as a team with the objective of maximizing their effectiveness in organizing the class for teaching and learning.

As described in Part 1, there are two roles for staff: the *learning manager*, who works intensively with one individual or group; and the *activity manager*, who works less intensively with several groups.

It does not matter whether the teacher or the TA takes on either of these roles. The learning manager concentrates on the work of individual students, or small groups, working intensively with them for short, specified periods of time. The activity manager will be focusing on the rest of the class – perhaps three or four groups. She or he will therefore be working with more students, but less intensively. This might involve working on activities that have already been taught and are being consolidated by the students. The activity manager will also be managing the routine and control of the class and dealing with any interruptions.

Room Management occurs during a period of time known as an *activity period*, usually involving small-group work. The 'job descriptions' of those roles are as follows. The *learning manager* concentrates on working with an individual or group on a teaching activity for 5–15 minutes. So in an hour it should be possible to arrange between 4 and 12 individual/group teaching sessions. The *activity manager* concentrates on the rest of the class, who will normally be arranged in groups of between 4 and 8. She or he will quickly move around keeping them busy and occupied.

Before the activity period the activity manager organizes the tasks and activities planned for each group to work on. During the activity period, the activity manager:

- ensures that each group member has appropriate materials/books/equipment;
- quickly prompts students to start working if necessary;

- supervises use of shared materials;
- moves around the groups to praise students who are busy;
- gives feedback on work;
- redirects group members who are not busy, helping to keep them on-task (these prompts will as far as possible be gestural or physical rather then verbal).

The learning manager:

- has a list or rota of students/groups and has everything necessary to work independently from the activity manager;
- asks each child/group on the list to come and work with them. The work for individuals/groups should last no longer than 15 minutes.

The room management planning sheet (on the following page) can be used as an additional support for this process.

Room management planning sheet

Date _____

	Group 1	Group 2	Group 3	Group 4	Group 5
Activity manager — Intended learning outcomes					
Task; Resources needed					
Role of activity manager					
Pupil/group →	1	2	3	4	5
Learning manager — Intended learning outcomes					
Task; Resources needed					
Role of learning manager					

Zoning

Zoning is a very simple way of organizing a classroom where there is more than one adult involved in teaching and organizing the class. The idea behind Zoning is that clarity – about who is doing what – is provided by clear definition as to where in the classroom different people are working. Thus, one person will be responsible, in the example in Figure 8.1, for groups A, B, C and D, while another will be responsible for groups E and F.

Things to think about for Zoning:

- Will the grouped zones comprise the same students as normally sit in these places, or will there be a rearrangement for the purpose of the session?
- What will be the balance of the groups?
- What will be the balance of the groups to the teacher/TA? Will the teacher take the larger group while the TA takes the smaller group?
- Will the students with special needs be placed in groups being overseen by the TA or the teacher?

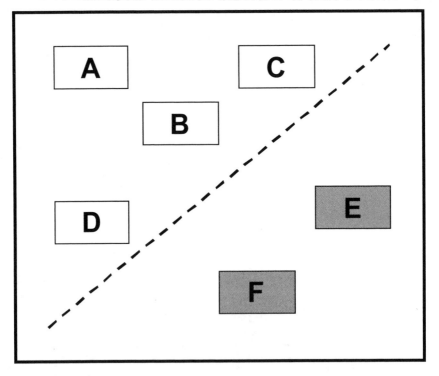

Figure 8.1 A possible Zoning group arrangement

In implementing Zoning procedures, it is useful also to think of the memory aid CHEER discussed on p. 71.

Reflective Teamwork

Reflective Teamwork uses a model underpinned by humanistic psychology to support teacher-TA teams to plan and evaluate teaching sessions together. Planning sessions should not take more than 15 minutes. To participate in this process most class teams will require training in areas such as:

- active listening;
- 'ground rules' to include avoiding put-downs, destructive criticism, and interrupting;
- empathic understanding;
- accepting alternative perspectives;
- using non-judgemental language;
- assertiveness;
- questioning techniques;
- giving feedback positively;
- problem-solving approaches;
- recognizing and valuing progress.

The Reflective Teamwork Planning Sheet on the following page enables teams to use the Reflective Teamwork planning structure for short-term planning and evaluating sessions where they work together. This model can be used on its own to improve communication and reflective practice as well as with the other two models.

Reflective Teamwork Planning Sheet

Planning together
15-minute planning meeting for teachers and TAs

Review of previous session

Minutes	Who	Content
2 {	TA	Two things that went well
	TA	Two things that we could improve
	TA	I am feeling ....
		because ....
1	Teacher	Summarize four things and feelings
2 {	Teacher	Two things that went well
	Teacher	Two things that we could improve
	Teacher	I am feeling ....
		because ....
1	TA	Summarize four things and feelings

Plan next session

Minutes	Who	Content
3		Brainstorm < Objectives / Activities
3	TA and teachers	Evaluate objectives and activities
3		Agree and write up plan

Both TA and teacher have access to all long-, medium- and short-term planning for that student/group of students being observed and come to the meeting having reflected on the previous session and read ahead with the planning.

9   CPD Activities

CPD involves change. Some time ago, two occupational psychologists, Nick Georgiades and Lynda Phillimore, coined a classic phrase that sums up the problems of trying to implement change in an organization after a member of staff has learned about new ideas which need implementing. Georgiades and Phillimore (1975) called this problem 'The myth of the hero innovator'.

The myth of the hero innovator is what has to be avoided in approaching any organizational change. For change to be effected, it is important that people:

- develop a critical mass – produce a team;
- work with the healthy parts of the system;
- work with managers.

In using the CPD activities on the following pages, whether just in your own classroom as teacher or TA, or in a school as a whole, it is worth considering these points. They are given again below with some suggestions about how to address them.

Develop a critical mass; produce a team   Let others in the school know about what you are doing. If people are able to work together they will feed off each other's enthusiasm, and be more able to resist the stress that comes with introducing change. Have as many informal meetings as possible. Involve the advisory and/or psychological service, who may be able to help – particularly with resources for training or with methods of evaluation.

Work with the healthy parts of the system

Don't try to convince those you know will vigorously resist this (or any) change. Your efforts would be better expended elsewhere and on something else.

Work with managers

One of the key findings to emerge from the research in Part 1 was the difficulty of finding time for planning, and the benefits to be gained for involving the headteacher and/ or senior management team, who would – for example – sometimes be able to find extra money for paid meeting time, or even offer to take classes themselves while meetings take place. It is essential for the head and senior staff to know at the outset what you are doing, and for them to be 'on-side'.

Room Management and Zoning CPD activity

The following pages give a set of activities that can be undertaken to assist in thinking about how Room Management and Zoning might be used in the classroom. The activities have been planned to fit into a training day.

These activities do not explain the Room Management and Zoning procedures in any more detail than they are outlined on pp. 45 to 50. Rather, the aim is to contextualize the procedures within the more general issues of classroom organization and learning needs. The aim is to help users to *reflect* on these models and how they may be used in their own classrooms.

In thinking about these issues we hope that it will be possible for users of the materials to adapt the advice on the use of the Room Management and Zoning models given in Chapter 4 to their own circumstances.

Guidelines

On the next few pages you will find:

- Reading: a case study in changing classroom organization – this is not a prescription, it is just an example;
- Reading: a list of some important considerations for learning and for classroom organization (also discussed more fully in Chapter 3);
- Activity: a blank template of a classroom;
- Activity: some 'furniture' to use as a template in thinking about the geography of the classroom.

What to do

 Read through the case study and the considerations about learning and classroom management in Chapter 3. Think about Room Management and Zoning and how these can help in organizing teacher-TA teamwork.

 Cut out the furniture on p. 137–8 and think about how you might reorganize your classroom using elements of Room Management and/or Zoning – consider especially the needs of the children in your class and the staff and resources available.

 Make notes for action about how you might reorganize your class and how teacher and TA will be working together to meet the needs of the class.

Reading: case study

The case study concerns changing classroom geography, and comes from Lucas and Thomas (2000).

Among many systems that I [Lucas] saw operating in classrooms was one that I felt might be of paramount importance – that of classroom layout – and which I adopted with a class of 26 KS2 children, of mixed abilities, ethnic and social backgrounds in an inner city school. There were three factors which influenced my choice of classroom layout. My experience with previous classes, particularly one in an educational priority area, had been that the so-called 'naughty children's table' would at times become a haven of respite for the child overcome by the demands of classroom and home life. Some children would ask to sit there. Secondly, like the teacher before me, I had not taken to the style of teaching children in small groups. Not only did I find children naturally gifted at confounding my carefully planned schedules but I was also sceptical as to the efficacy with which teachers teach and children learn within this system of organization. It seemed that such seating arrangements did not always enhance the style of learning. Thirdly, I wished to re-integrate a student with a statement of special educational needs into her own class. Thus my aims were to match the children's learning, and my teaching, to the classroom geography. As teachers may draw from a range of teaching strategies during their working days the flexibility of any classroom arrangements remains of the utmost importance.

I began reorganising the classroom by getting rid of any furniture I considered superfluous. The children's tables (all two-seaters) were moved out to the walls so that they formed a 'ring' around the perimeter of the room, with their chairs facing outwards towards the walls. I moved the carpet to the centre and positioned four units (one bookcase, two display units and a woodwork bench) at angles on the carpet corners. This was the basic structure of the room. It was very simple and very spacious. [The reorganized classroom is shown in the figure on p. 134.]

I set up containers on one display table for the children's work books, leaving their tidy trays available for the maths equipment and, more crucially, promoting the importance of their work. Throughout the year the children were responsible for making covers for all of their exercise books. Thus, the books were personalized and displayed.

On the first day of term I explained why I had done such an odd thing to our new classroom. I told the children that we would use the carpet (the centre of the room) as a meeting place/group work area where we would talk and discuss activities and then move out to the walls to work. Before we left the carpet (or base) we would discuss the nature of the day/session, whether or not it would require moving the tables into groups, who would be talking (in collaborative work) and so on. In this way, an agreement was reached about who was doing what – roles were made explicit. This notion of moving *away* from the centre of the room also produced an air of industry.

One necessary rule came from the children: in sessions devoted to individual work any one child had the right to ask for total silence. I was uncertain about this at the beginning as I did not want to deny purposeful discussion. However, this was the consensus of the class which perhaps reflected children's perceptions of the workplace. We also decided we would agree on a time to meet back on the carpet to show the work that had been done. This may have motivated some while promoting pride in others. The system was tried for a month and reviewed; as it turned out, the reaction was positive.

During the first week, Susan, a child with a statement of special educational needs, found it hard to adjust to the new system. She had learning and slight coordination difficulties and was easily distracted. She had no special place near me, largely because I had no fixed place either. She was part of the circle of children. However, after only a short time, there was a dramatic change in her attitude to herself, her class and her work. She was no longer an outsider but now an insider – part of the circle. During showing times, she would proudly hold up her work and receive encouragement from her classmates. Perhaps it helped them to understand what she was doing and helped her to feel part of the group.

There were other benefits in meeting the children's needs for conditions conducive to individual work and preventing special needs arising.

1   There was less possibility for the emergence of a group of children 'setting up camp' on a group table (a familiar occurrence in grouped classrooms). It is much harder to set up camp in a row of tables than a group. Taking this one step further, it is difficult to form hierarchies in a circle.

2   It is easier to glance up and see if the teacher is watching you than to have to turn around to do so. The organization of many classrooms fosters a dependency on the teacher for control, rather than encouraging self control. With this classroom layout the teacher is no longer the focus – releasing her from 'raised-eyebrow and glare' duty.

3   It met the children's needs for a clear, meaningful and workable system.

4   Conditions for learning effectively were met. Unless doing group work, most adults would choose to work in conditions of least distraction. Why, then, do we persist in asking children to concentrate when they are seated at groups of tables designed for social interaction? This is not to negate the importance of children's talk in learning, merely to think more clearly about its role. The noise level in the reorganized classroom was consistently quiet, sometimes disconcertingly so. On reflection, it may simply have been that the new classroom layout had put a spanner in a popular but not invariably ideal system and the children were now given a chance to concentrate.

An interesting spin-off to the new organization was that playtime became less popular. Motivation had clearly increased.

The following page shows the reorganized classroom. (Each little circle represents a child in their 'home' place.)

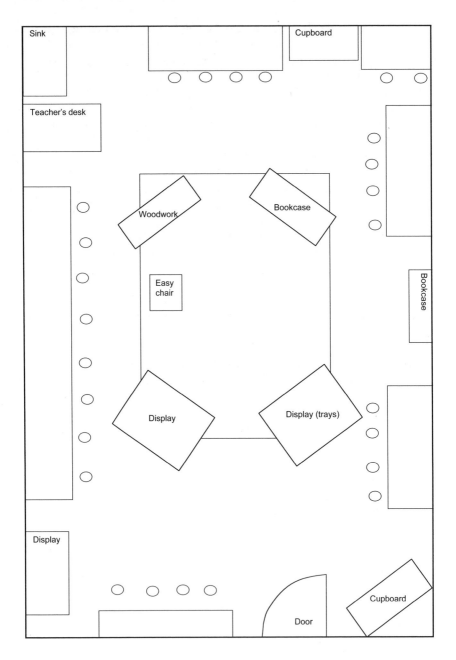

Reading: Learning and classroom organization

Individual needs	Group needs
When children learn, what do they need?	What do effective teachers do? Research shows that they …
Regular opportunity for teaching and learning	Regularly circulate
	Provide feedback to children on work and behaviour
Learning little and often (called 'distributed practice' in the jargon) – for example, 8 × 5 minute sessions are better than a 1 × 40 minute session	
	Plan transitions – minimize periods of disruption and confusion
Absence from distraction. This might be achieved through regrouping the children or having a section of the room available for individualized teaching away from doors, windows, etc.	
	Maintain flow – minimize interruptions to flow (e.g. with nagging, bursting in on a group with a question)
As much help as possible from a teacher or TA. Provide as much help as necessary, making sure the work is successfully undertaken, so that the child finishes feeling good.	
All these are provided by a learning manager	All these are provided by an activity manager

Basic classroom shape.
Using an A4 sheet of paper, draw in door/s
and windows as in this example

Activity

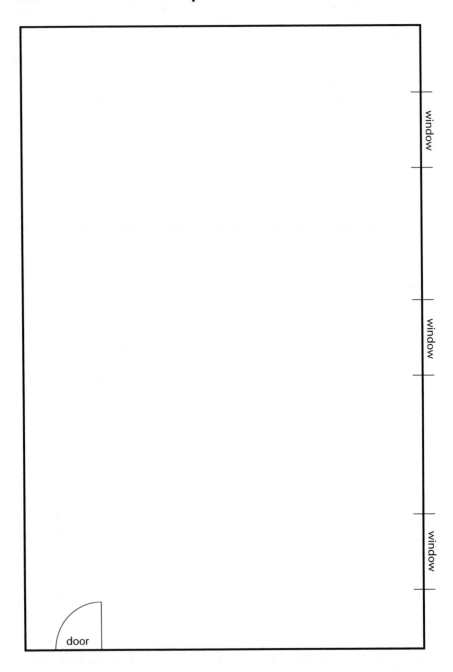

Activity

The classroom 'mapping tool' is based on a class of 28 children, with two children to each table. There are six extra tables for display, artwork etc. Some cupboards and other furniture are also provided. This is not supposed to be exactly like your own classroom. It is just a way of thinking about how you might arrange children and the geography of the classroom to best effect.

Tables

Cupboards

Bookcases

Teacher's desk   TA's work base

Reflective Teamwork CPD activities

These activities are designed for all teachers and TAs in a school who may be introducing new ways of working. The activities aim to:

- improve reflective listening skills in teachers and TAs;
- strengthen relationships and build a sense of team;
- support effective evaluation and planning of teaching.

Clearly, it is important throughout that when discussing teamwork and team behaviours in school, names or easily identifiable individuals are not used as examples for public discussion!

Activity 1

This is a brainstorming activity to get teachers and TAs to reflect on their own ideas of effective teacher-TA partnership and teamworking.

1   Teachers and TAs are randomly assigned to small groups and asked to record their free-flowing thoughts onto flipchart paper.
2   Small groups feed back to the whole group.
3   The whole group reads the sheet 'Some key principles for effective teacher-TA teamwork'. The group feedback is discussed in the context of these ideas (which represent a summary of our review of the research literature given in Chapter 2).

Some key principles for effective teacher-TA teamwork

1   Senior managers demonstrate commitment to teamwork, which might include a vision for successful classroom teamwork, non-contact time, venues for training and meetings, and review and feedback on performance.

2   Classroom teams are clear that they are a team and value positive interdependence.

3   There is a recognition that team-building skills can be learned. Training and ongoing support might include areas such as effective communication, problem-solving and dealing with controversy.

4   Team members have a strong role in defining effective practice for their classroom teams.

5   Teachers and TAs have opportunities to reflect on, share and agree their common aims, goals and roles within the team.

6   The team knows what it is expected to deliver. Both the teacher and TA are committed to this.

7   Goals relate to work undertaken in the classroom and also to team processes.

8   TAs are allocated to work with a limited number of teachers so that they can spend time getting to know each other.

9   Classroom teams have good communication systems. TAs and teachers have time to plan and evaluate together.

10   Meetings are carefully structured, with clear roles and opportunities for all to give views, regardless of status.

11   Time for teachers and TAs to meet outside teaching time is accounted for in pay structures and cover costs.

12   Teachers and TAs participate in at least some joint training.

13   Teams feel empowered and use their autonomy effectively to solve problems.

14   Classroom teams self-evaluate regularly against joint and individual performance targets.

15   Teams frequently celebrate.

Activity 2

This activity, taken from transactional analysis, is intended to demonstrate how a more equal partnership between teachers and TAs is based on valuing different perspectives and experiences.

1   Give a copy of the handout for Activity 2 to every teacher and TA.
2   Ask them to imagine that 'I' is a teacher and that 'you' is a TA. In each box the participants describe the type of relationship that would follow if the attitudes described in each box were held by the teacher. For example, in the top left hand box, if the teacher felt that they were 'OK', but that the TA was 'not OK', what would be the ensuing relationship?
3   Get them to compare notes with a partner.
4   Feed back as a whole group. What are the implications of this activity for the relationships between teachers and TAs in schools?

Handout

Cooperation and mutual respect – a transaction analysis model	
I'm OK. You're not OK.	I'm OK. You're OK.
I'm not OK. You're OK.	I'm not OK. You're not OK.

Activity 3

This activity makes explicit some of the skills and attitudes that are essential for reflective listening and teamwork.

1. Give out a copy of the Chinese symbol for listening shown below. Discuss the different parts of the symbol.
2. Ask mixed small groups of teachers and TAs to flipchart the elements of good and bad listening.
3. Get each small group to feed these back to the rest.
4. Give out a copy of the sheet: 'What makes a good listener?' Discuss any elements that were missed.
5. Give out a copy of the sheet: 'Cooperative teamwork'. Discuss any points.

Handout

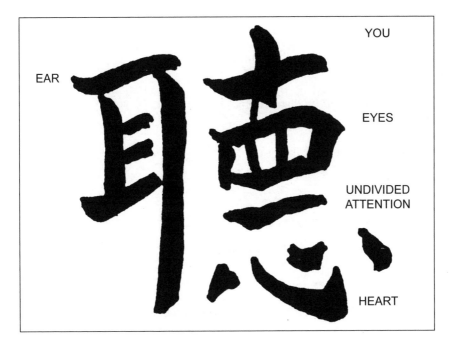

The Chinese symbol for listening

Handout

What makes a good listener?

- Commitment to listening

- Not put off by distractions

- Focuses on speaker

- Sensitive to feelings

- Concentrates on the meaning of what's being said, not just the words

- Clarifies, reflects back to check has picked up the correct meaning

- Listens with the whole body – good eye contact, non-verbal feedback, smiles, nods head appropriately

- Summarizes what has been said

Handout

Cooperative teamwork

Teams are working cooperatively when ...

Groundrules

- Language is respectful and people avoid put-downs and destructive criticism

- There is space for everyone to speak with no one interrupting or 'hogging' meetings

Attitude

- There is an openness to teamwork and shared responsibility

- People are willing to explore the points of view of others

- People are willing to accept compromise where appropriate

- No one sees themselves as more important than anyone else

Language

- Language used is assertive (not aggressive, manipulative or passive)

- Questions are used to elicit more information and to clarify, not to limit or direct discussions

- There is an absence of judgemental or opinionated language

- There is lots of acknowledgement of the achievements of others

- People say 'thank you' regularly

Body language

- People are conscious of the defensive body language of others and respond with empathy and a problem-solving approach

Activity 4

This activity explores ways of asking open questions that enable people to keep talking if they dry up in team planning time. It is useful for supporting people to be non-directive during listening time.

1 Give out a copy of the sheet: 'Open Questions'. Go over the various points contained on the sheet.
2 Ask groups five closed questions that they know they normally use in school.
3 Get the groups to reformulate these questions as open questions.
4 Discuss the activity as a whole group. Are there some questions that need to be phrased as closed questions? What is the effect of rephrasing closed questions as open questions?

Open questions

Open questions can explore a problem more fully:
- Tell me about that ...
- Describe ...
- In what way ...
- Give me an example ...

Open questions can also be used to ask about feelings:
- How did you feel when ... ?
- What did you feel about ... ?
- What are your feelings now ... ?

Open questions can be used to ask about what someone did and what their opinions are:
- What did you do when ... ?
- And after that?
- What do you think about ... ?

Questions to avoid:

1   *Leading questions.* This can be an undercover way of trying to influence the speaker:
- You would agree with me that ... wouldn't you?
- Do you think that you did that because you were upset?
- Would it have been better if ... do you think?

2   *Multi-choice questions.* These are like closed questions, e.g.:
- Would you prefer to do ... or ... ?

3   *Multiple questions.* Asking several questions together without waiting for a response. The speaker will generally answer the easiest question only.

4   *Asking a question and answering it yourself.*
- Why do you think she did that? Maybe because she was depressed.

5   *Poorly-timed questions.* Especially ones which interrupt the speaker or stop them from expressing an emotion.

Activity 5

This activity aims to explore the differences between assertive, aggressive and passive behaviour in order to enable team members to be more aware of the various helpful and unhelpful behaviours that take place in teams.

1   Ask three small groups to flipchart what they understand by either 'assertive behaviour', 'aggressive behaviour' or 'passive behaviour'.
2   Get each group to feed back to the rest.
3   Give out the sheets; What is assertiveness?; and 'Unhelpful behaviours for effective teamwork'. Discuss elements of these that may have been missed.
4   What can be done structurally in school in order to support people to be more assertive and less aggressive or passive?

Handout

What is assertiveness?

Assertiveness is a way of behaving which encourages clear and honest expression of feelings and views (whether they are positive or negative) whilst also respecting the feelings of others. It is essential for effective team-work.

Being assertive involves:

- Recognizing one's own needs and asking openly and directly for them to be met.

- Recognizing the rights and needs of others.

- Relating to other people in an open and honest way.

- Feeling responsible for and in control of your own actions.

- Being prepared to compromise and negotiate a win/win solution.

- Being able to resolve problems and disputes in a way that feels comfortable and fair to everyone involved.

Being able to do all of these things will still not guarantee that people get everything that they feel they need, but it will guarantee that people are able to handle situations with confidence and do their best to arrive at a fair resolution.

Handout

Unhelpful behaviours for effective teamwork

Aggressiveness
Examples of aggressive behaviour include:

- Expressing feelings and opinions in a way that punishes, threatens or puts other people down.
- Disregarding the rights of others.
- Aiming to get one's own way no matter what.

Passivity
Examples of passive behaviour include:

- Allowing others to take advantage.
- Not standing up for your own rights.
- Leaving others to make decisions by avoiding responsibility for making your own choices.
- Not taking control where needed/appropriate.
- Describing yourself as a helpless victim of unfairness and injustice.
- Believing that luck or wishing hard enough will make things happen.

Manipulation
Examples of manipulative behaviour include:

- Hinting and asking indirectly for needs to be met.
- Trying to get needs met by making people feel guilty or beholden in some way.

Activity 6

This activity supports adults in schools (whatever their perceived status) to say no.

1. In pairs, get people to use their active listening skills to share times when they have found it difficult to say no.
2. Give out sheet 'Saying no'. Go over the points and discuss.

Handout

Saying no

■ Keep the reply short – avoid rambling and justifications.

■ Simply say

　■ 'No, I don't want to'.

　■ 'I prefer not to'.

　■ 'I'd rather not'.

　■ 'I'm not happy to'.

■ Do not invent an excuse.

■ Don't apologize profusely.

■ Honestly state your limitations.

■ Make sure your body language and tone of voice is as relaxed and confident as possible.

■ Acknowledge your feelings.

■ Don't repeat your refusal.

10 A Toolkit for Classroom Research

Most classroom research is about trying to understand in clearer detail some aspect of classroom activity. The kind of research undertaken for the projects reported in this book was a particular kind that *evaluated* a set of changes that were introduced to the classroom.

This type of research is often called *action research*. This simply means research that is done in context and that involves the active participation of those who are at the 'sharp end' – in this case the teacher and the TA. It accepts the need for change in the design of the research as the project proceeds: nothing is set in stone.

The evaluative action research reported in this book shares features that you may repeat when you undertake your own research. You will want to know whether what you are doing is working, and whether there are ways of improving it. Like us, you will therefore need to answer a number of questions about:

- what is happening when you introduce your change;
- what effects your change is having on the classroom;
- whether the change is helping you to meet the goals that you set yourself;
- whether you can change things to improve the programme you have initiated;
- if there are ways that you can spread your knowledge to others in your school, or colleagues in other schools.

These research questions would suggest a range of evaluation tools. These might include

- student questionnaires;
- interviews with adults involved in the programme;
- structured observation of lessons.

We now give adapted versions of the tools used in our research in the hope that you may be able to use them in evaluating your own changes. Like all tools, they are capable of adaptation. They are not blueprints. In other words, they are offered as guidance for your own situation. They are not meant to be followed rigidly, though you may wish to use them as they are.

Student Questionnaires

The student questionnaire is designed to answer the question 'Do these methods have an impact on effective inclusive practice in classrooms?'

The questionnaire provides a brief audit of inclusive classrooms. It asks students a number of questions relating to their feelings of being included by their teacher, TA and their classmates. It is adapted from the CSIE *Index of Inclusion* (Booth *et al.* 2002), which is intended to be used as a diagnostic tool. The questionnaire is relatively easy to score. Each of the indicators scores 2 for a 'yes', 0 for a 'no' and 1 for 'a bit'.

The questionnaire can be given before and after any change is introduced to try to gauge whether the change has had any effect on the attitudes of the students.

Questionnaire 1

What I think about my primary school

Age..............   Class...............   Boy/Girl

A: My teacher	Yes	A bit	No
My teacher likes to listen to my ideas			
My teacher helps me with my work			
I think my teacher's classroom rules are fair			
If I have a problem I can tell my teacher			
Sometimes my teacher lets me choose what work to do			
My teacher tells me when I have done something well			

Questionnaire 1 cont.

B: Our teaching assistant	Yes	A bit	No
Our teaching assistant likes to listen to my ideas			
Our teaching assistant helps me with my work			
If I have a problem I can tell our teaching assistant			
Sometimes our teaching assistant lets me choose what work to do			
Our teaching assistant tells me when I have done something well			

Questionnaire 1 cont.

C: My class	Yes	A bit	No
People in my class like to listen to my ideas			
I help my friends with their work when they get stuck			
My friends help me with my work when I get stuck			
I get on with my work without wasting time			
Most other children in my class get on with their work without wasting time			
In my class children help each other			
Sometimes I do class work with other children in a small group or in a pair			
I think writing targets for the term helps my work to improve			
Children in my class say nice things about me			

Questionnaire 2

Secondary student questionnaire

Age..............   Form...............   Boy/Girl

A: My ....teacher (please put the subject here)	Yes	A bit	No
My teacher likes to listen to my ideas			
My teacher helps me with my work			
I think my teacher's rules are fair			
If I have a problem I can tell my teacher			
Sometimes my teacher lets me choose what work to do			
My teacher tells me when I have done something well			

Questionnaire 2 cont.

B: Our teaching assistant in	Yes	A bit	No
Our teaching assistant likes to listen to my ideas			
Our teaching assistant helps me with my work			
If I have a problem I can tell our teaching assistant			
Sometimes our teaching assistant lets me choose what work to do			
Our teaching assistant tells me when I have done something well			

Questionnaire 2 cont.

C: My class in	Yes	A bit	No
People in my class like to listen to my ideas			
I help my friends with their work when they get stuck			
My friends help me with my work when I get stuck			
I get on with my work without wasting time			
Most other students in my class get on with their work without wasting time			
In my class students help each other			
Sometimes I do class work with other students in a small group or in a pair			
I think writing targets for the term helps my work to improve			
Students in my class say nice things about me			

Student questionnaire score sheet 1

What I think about my primary school

Class Score Sheet
Enter the total of the scores for each question for the class, e.g. if 18 children in the class think that their teacher likes to listen to their ideas (yes) and 3 children think that their teacher likes to listen to their ideas a bit, the score would be 18 × 2 (i.e. 36) + 3 = 39 for question 1.

Average Age...............   **Class...............**

No. in class................

A: My teacher	Score
My teacher likes to listen to my ideas	
My teacher helps me with my work	
I think my teacher's classroom rules are fair	
If I have a problem I can tell my teacher	
Sometimes my teacher lets me choose what work to do	
My teacher tells me when I have done something well	

B: Our teaching assistant	Score
Our teaching assistant likes to listen to my ideas	
Our teaching assistant helps me with my work	
If I have a problem I can tell our teaching assistant	
Sometimes our teaching assistant lets me choose what work to do	
Our teaching assistant tells me when I have done something well	

C: My class	Score
People in my class like to listen to my ideas	
I help my friends with their work when they get stuck	
My friends help me with my work when I get stuck	
I get on with my work without wasting time	
Most other children in my class get on with their work without wasting time	
In my class children help each other	
Sometimes I do class work with other children in a small group or in a pair	
I think writing targets for the term helps my work to improve	
Children in my class say nice things about me	

Student questionnaire score sheet 2

Secondary student questionnaire score sheet

Class Score Sheet
Enter the total of the scores for each question for the class, e.g. if 18 children in the class think that their teacher likes to listen to their ideas (yes) and 3 children think that their teacher likes to listen to their ideas a bit, the score would be 18 × 2 (i.e. 36) + 3 = 39 for question 1.

Average Age............... Class............... Subject........................

No. in class.................

A: My teacher	Score
My teacher likes to listen to my ideas	
My teacher helps me with my work	
I think my teacher's classroom rules are fair	
If I have a problem I can tell my teacher	
Sometimes my teacher lets me choose what work to do	
My teacher tells me when I have done something well	

B: Our teaching assistant	Score
Our teaching assistant likes to listen to my ideas	
Our teaching assistant helps me with my work	
If I have a problem I can tell our teaching assistant	
Sometimes our teaching assistant lets me choose what work to do	
Our teaching assistant tells me when I have done something well	

C: My class	Score
People in my class like to listen to my ideas	
I help my friends with their work when they get stuck	
My friends help me with my work when I get stuck	
I get on with my work without wasting time	
Most other students in my class get on with their work without wasting time	
In my class students help each other	
Sometimes I do class work with other students in a small group or in a pair	
I think writing targets for the term helps my work to improve	
Students in my class say nice things about me	

Conducting interviews

One of the most valuable ways of finding out about classroom experiences from the point of view of the participants is simply to ask them about those experiences in an interview.

There are a number of different kinds of interview: *structured interviews*, which are precisely delivered sets of questions, with little or no deviation; *semi-structured interviews*, which have a set of core issues to be covered, but which allow a certain amount of variation to permit the following of interesting lines; and *unstructured interviews*, which have no preconceived format and which follow the issues raised by the respondent.

It was felt that in researching the topic under study here, semi-structured interviews would be most relevant and valuable, and it was these that were used in gaining most of the interview data reported in this book.

It is important to remember a number of things when interviewing. Establishing a rapport with respondents is important, particularly children. Open-ended and non-directive questions should be used, the researcher following up interesting avenues that emerge and following the respondent's interests or concerns. The respondent is able to give a fuller picture and shares more closely in the direction the interview takes, including introducing issues the researcher had not considered. In this sense, the respondent can be thought of as 'the expert' and allowed to tell their own 'story'. An interview schedule should be prepared, but the researcher should be guided rather than dictated by it.

Here is a summary of some issues for consideration when interviewing children or adults.

Interviewing children

- Create a rapport.
- Explain your purpose – allow 'opt out'.
- Be accepting.
- Be 'on a level' with them – physically as well as metaphorically.
- Use open rather than closed questions.
- Make notes after, not during, the interview.

Interviewing other adults

- Same considerations as for children, plus …
- Have an interview schedule that outlines three or four key areas to cover.
- Explain in more detail how the findings of the research are to be used and procedures for making transcripts anonymous.

Questions for adults might include

- How did you put into practice the principles that were outlined in the training sessions?
- How did the intervention affect your planning?
- How did the intervention affect teamworking with your TA or teacher?
- How did the intervention affect the role clarity of the TA and teacher?
- How was the model different from your usual practice?
- What has the effect been on the students?
- What were the positives?
- What were the negatives?

Classroom observation of student engagement

For our research, the observation and analysis of student engagement was designed to answer the question: 'What is the effect of Room Management, Zoning and Reflective Teamwork on the quality of learning and teaching?'

'Engagement' refers to the extent that students are on-task during any teaching period. It provides a useful measure of how well organized and industrious the class is. One reason for this choice is that this measure has been used in other research into Room Management and Zoning procedures. Although it has its obvious weaknesses, it has proved to be a robust and reliable measure of classroom activity with much research to show that engagement rates relate solidly to achievement.

Instructions for collecting data

1   Decide on how you are going to assess engagement or 'on-task-ness' – how will you judge whether students are doing what they are supposed to be doing? Make a note of the kinds of activities and behaviours that count as on-task and off-task.

2   Since 1 is harder than it sounds, have a *pilot* in which you observe two or three students in the classroom for a short trial period and try to judge – using the criteria you noted in 1 – whether the students are on- or off-task. Refine your criteria ready for your actual data collection.

3   Identify ten or so students for data collection – a mixture of boys/ girls, of different abilities. You might wish specifically to include in your data collection students with whom you experience particular difficulty.

4   For a period of 20 minutes complete the student engagement tally for the ten students, using the 'student engagement observation sheet' provided.

5   Every minute look at each student quickly in turn and note whether they are on- or off-task. Put a tick if the student is on-task and a cross if not.

6   For each student calculate the percentage of time on-task (number of ticks divided by total number of tallies × 100). For example, if a student obtains 16 ticks out of a possible 20, then 16/20 × 100 means the student was on task for 80 per cent of the time. Note your results on the 'Student engagement score sheet'.

7   Take readings before and after the change to your working practice has been implemented and plot your results on a graph similar to those shown in this book.

Student engagement observation sheet

Student	1 min	2 min	3 min	4 min	5 min	6 min	7 min	8 min	9 min	10 min	11 min	12 min	13 min	14 min	15 min	16 min	17 min	18 min	19 min	20 min	Student

Student engagement score sheet

School/class..

Student	% on task baseline	% on task post-intervention

References

Ball, S. J. (1997) Policy sociology and critical social research: a personal view of recent education policy and policy research, *British Educational Research Journal*, 23(2): 257–74.

Bantel, K. and Jackson, S. (1989) Top management and innovations in banking: does the composition of the top team make a difference? *Strategic Management Journal*, 10: 107–24.

Barber, M. and Brighouse, T. (1992) *Partners in Change: Enhancing the Teaching Profession*. London: IPPR.

Barker, D. (1980) *TA and Training*. Aldershot: Gower.

Baron, R., Kerr, N. and Miller, N. (1992) *Group Process, Group Decision, Group Action*. Pacific Grove, CA: Brooks/Cole.

Becker, W., Madsen, C., Arnold, C. and Thomas, D. (1967) The contingent use of teacher attention and praise in reducing classroom behaviour problems, *Journal of Special Education*, 1: 287–307.

Belbin, R.M. (1981) *Management Teams*. London: Heinemann.

Belbin, R.M. (1993) *Team Roles at Work*. London: Butterworth.

Bennett, N. and Blundell, D. (1983) Quantity and quality of work in rows and classroom groups, *Educational Psychology*, 3(2): 93–105.

Blatchford, P., Martin, C., Moriarty, V., Bassett, B. and Goldstein, H. (2001) *Pupil Adult Ratio Differences and Educational Progress over Key Stage One*. London: Institute of Education, University of London.

Booth, T. (1996) A perspective on inclusion from England, *Cambridge Journal of Education*, 26(1): 87–98.

Booth, T., Ainscow, M., Black-Hawkins, K., Vaughan, M. and Shaw, L. (2002) *Index for Inclusion: Developing Learning and Participation in Schools*. Bristol: Centre for Studies on Inclusive Education (CSIE).

Bowers, T. (1997) Supporting special needs in the mainstream classroom – children's perceptions of the adult role, *Child Care, Health and Development*, 23: 217–32.

Bredson, P. (1989) Redefining leadership and the roles of school principals: responses to changes in the working life of teachers. Paper presented at the Annual Meeting of the American Educational Research Association, San Francisco.

Brennan, W. K. (1982) *Special Education in Mainstream Schools: The Search for Quality.* Stratford upon Avon: National Council for Special Education.

Brophy, J. (1982) *Classroom Organisation and Management.* Unpublished paper, Michigan State University (ERIC, ED 218257).

Buchanan, D.A. and Huczynski, A.A. (1985) *Organisational Behaviour.* Englewood Cliffs, NJ: Prentice-Hall.

Carpenter, J. and Hewstone, M. (1996) Shared learning for doctors and social workers: evaluation of a programme, *The British Journal of Social Work,* 26(2): 239–57.

Clayton, T. (1990) The training needs of special welfare assistants: what do heads, classteachers and the assistants themselves regard as important? *Educational and Child Psychology,* 7(1): 44–51.

Clayton, T. (1993) From domestic helper to 'assistant teacher' – the changing role of the British classroom assistant, *European Journal of Special Needs Education,* 8(1): 32–44.

Clift, P., Cleave, S. and Griffin, M. (1980) *The Aims, Role and Deployment of Staff in the Nursery.* Windsor: NFER.

Cohen, E. G. (1976) Problems and prospects of teaming, *Educational Research Quarterly,* 1(2): 49–63.

Coles, E. and Blunden, R. (1979) *The Establishment and Maintenance of a Ward-Based Activity Period within a Mental Handicapped Hospital,* Research Report no. 8, Mental Handicap in Wales Applied Research Unit, University of South Wales, Cardiff.

Conley, S., Schmidle, T. and Shedd, J. (1988) Teacher participation in the management of school systems, *Teachers College Record,* 90: 259–80.

Coopersmith, S. (1967) *The Antecedents of Self Esteem.* San Francisco: Freeman.

Crom, S. and France, H. (1996) Teamwork brings breakthrough improvements in quality and climate, *Quality Progress,* 29(3): 39–42.

CSIE (Centre for Studies on Inclusive Education) (1995) *Checklist for Inclusion: Developing Schools' Policies to Include Disabled Children.* Bristol: Centre for Studies on Inclusive Education.

Delefes, P. and Jackson, B. (1972) Teacher student interaction as a function of location in the classroom, *Psychology in the Schools,* 9: 119–23.

DES (Department of Education and Science) (1967) *Children and their Primary Schools: A Report of the Central Advisory Council for Education (England),* vol. 1 (the Plowden Report). London: HMSO.

Deutsch, M. (1973) Equity, equality and need: what determines which value will be used as the basis of distributive justice? *Journal of Social Issues,* 31: 137–49.

DeVault, M.L., Harnischfeger, A. and Wiley, D.E. (1977) *Curricula, Personnel Resources and Grouping Strategies.* St Ann, MO: ML Group for Policy Studies in Education, Central Midwestern Regional Lab.

DfEE (Department for Education and Employment) (1997) *Higher Eduction in the Learning Society* (the Dearing Report). London: HMSO.

DfEE (Department for Education and Employment) (2000) *Statistics of Education, Schools in England.* London: DfEE.

DfES (Department for Education and Skills) (2002) *Time for Standards: Reforming the School Workforce.* London: DfES.

DfES (Department for Education and Skills) (2003a) *Statistics of Education, Schools in England.* London: DfES.

DfES (Department for Education and Skills) (2003b) *Developing the Role of School Support Staff.* London: DfES.

DfES (Department for Education and Skills) (2004a) *School Support Staff Training and Development.* London: DfES.

DfES (Department for Education and Skills) (2004b) *Statistics of Education, Schools in England.* London: DfES.

Doyle, W. (1986) Classroom organisation and management, in R.M.W. Travers (ed.) *Handbook of Research on Teaching*, 3rd edn, pp. 392–431. New York: Macmillan.

Drucker, P. (1994) The age of social transformation, *The Atlantic Monthly*, November.

Eyres, I., Cable, C., Hancock, R. and Turner, J. (2004) 'Whoops, I forgot David': children's perceptions of the adults who work in their classrooms, *Early Years*, 24(2): 149–62.

Farrell, P., Balshaw, M. and Polat, F. (1999) *The Management, Role and Training of Learning Support Assistants.* Norwich: DfEE.

Firth, J. (1983) Experiencing uncertainty: organisational lessons from the clinic, *Personnel Review*, 12(2): 11–15.

Fish, J. (1985) *Special Education: The Way Ahead.* Milton Keynes: Open University Press.

Frelow, R.D., Charry, J. and Freilich, B. (1974) Academic progress and behavioural changes in low achieving students, *Journal of Educational Research*, 67: 263–6.

French, N.K. and Chopra, R.V. (1999) Parent perspectives on the roles of paraprofessionals, *Journal of the Association for Persons with Severe Handicaps*, 24: 259–72.

Galagan, P. (1986) Work teams that work, *Training and Development Journal*, 11: 33–5.

Galton, M., Simon, B. and Croll, P. (1980) *Inside the Primary Classroom.* London: Routledge & Kegan Paul.

Garvin, D. (1988) *Managing Quality: The Strategic and Competitive Edge.* New York: Free Press.

Geen, A.G. (1985) Team teaching in the secondary schools of England and Wales, *Educational Review*, 37(1): 29–38.

Georgiades, N.J. and Phillimore, L. (1975) The myth of the hero-innovator and alternative strategies for organizational change, in C.C. Kiernan and F.P. Woodford (eds) *Behaviour Modification with the Severely Retarded.* Amsterdam: Associated Scientific Publishers.

Georgiades, W. and Keefe, J. (1992) A second-generation design: the learning environments consortium, in National Association of Secondary School Principals (ed.) *A Leaders Guide to School Restructuring: A Special Report of the NASSP Commission on Restructuring,* PR.15–22. Reston, VA: NA SSP.

Gerber, S.B., Finn, J.D., Achilles, C.M. and Boyd-Zaharias, J. (2001) Teacher aides and students' academic achievement, *Educational Evaluation and Policy Analysis,* 23(2): 123–44.

Gewirtz, S. and Ball, S. (2000) From 'welfarism' to 'new managerialism': shifting discourses of school headship in the education marketplace, *Discourse: Studies in the Cultural Politics of Education,* 21(3): 253–68.

Giangreco, M., Edelman, S., Luiselli, T. and MacFarland, S. (1997) Helping or hovering? Effects of instructional assistant proximity on students with disabilities, *Exceptional Children,* 64: 7–18.

Giangreco, M.F., Edelman, S.W., Broer, S.M. and Doyle, M.B. (2001) Paraprofessional support of students with disabilities: literature from the past decade, *Exceptional Children,* 68(1): 45–63.

Gibb, J. (1961) Defensive communication, *Journal of Communication,* 11: 141–8.

Gladstein, D. (1984) Groups in context: a model of task group effectiveness, *Administrative Science Quarterly,* 29: 499–517.

Goleman, D. (1998) *Working with Emotional Intelligence.* London: Bloomsbury.

Gump, P. (1969) Intra-setting analysis: the third grade classroom as a special but instructive case, in E.P. Willems and H.L. Rush (eds) *Naturalistic Viewpoints in Psychological Research.* New York: Holt, Rinehart & Winston.

Hackman, J. (1987) The design of work teams, in J. Lorsch (ed.) *Handbook of Organisational Behaviour,* pp. 315–42. New York: Prentice Hall.

Hackman, J.R. and Morris, C. (1975) Group tasks, group interaction process and group performance effectiveness: a review and proposed integration, in L. Berkowitz (ed.) *Advances in Experimental Social Psychology,* vol. 12, pp. 530–84. New York: Academic Press.

Hall, J. and Williams, M. (1996) A comparison of decision making performance in established and ad hoc groups, *Journal of Personality and Social Psychology,* 3: 214–22.

Hancock, R., Swann, W., Marr, A., Turner, J. and Cable, C. (2002) *Classroom Assistants in Primary Schools: Employment and Deployment,* Report for ESRC project R000237803. Milton Keynes: The Open University.

Handy, C.B. (1993) *Understanding Organisations.* London: Penguin.

Handy, C.B. (1995) *The Empty Raincoat.* London: Arrow Business Books.

Hardaker, M. and Ward, B. (1987) Getting things done: how to make a team work, *Harvard Business Review*, 65: 112–19.

Hargreaves, D.H. (1972) *Interpersonal Relations and Education*. London: Routledge & Kegan Paul.

Hart, B. and Risley, T. (1976) Environmental reprogramming: implications for the severely handicapped, unpublished paper. Kansas: Center for Applied Behavior Analysis.

Hatton, E.J. (1985) Team teaching and teacher orientation to work: implications for the pre-service and in-service education of teachers, *Journal of Education for Teaching*, 11(3): 228–44.

Henkin, A.B. and Wanat, C.L. (1994) Problem-solving teams and the improvement of organisational performance in schools, *School Organisation*, 14(2): 121.

HMI (2002) *Teaching Assistants in Primary Schools: An Evaluation of the Quality and Impact of their Work: A report by HMI*, HMI 434. London: Ofsted.

Hoffman, L. (1979) Applying experimental research on group problem-solving to organisations, *Journal of Applied Behavioural Sciences*, 15: 375–91.

Honey, P. and Mumford, A. (1986) *The Manual of Learning Styles*. Maidenhead: Peter Honey, Ardingly House.

Horst, M. *et al.* (1995) St Joseph's Community Health Centre model of community, *Health and Social Care in the Community*, 3: 33–42.

Hrekow, P. and Barrow, G. (1993) Developing a system of inclusive education for pupils with behavioural difficulties, *Pastoral Care*, June: 6–13.

Imber, M. and Neidt, W.A. (1990) Teachers' efficacy at work, in P. Reyes (ed.) *Teachers and Their Workplace*. Beverly Hills, CA: Sage.

Inglese, J. (1996) Special teachers? Perceptions of the special expertise required for effective special educational needs teaching and advisory work, *Support for Learning*, 11(2): 83–7.

Janis, I. (1983) *Victims of Groupthink*. Boston, MA: Houghton Mifflin.

Johnson, D.W. and Johnson, F.P. (2000) *Joining Together: Group Theory and Group Skills*. Needham Heights, MA: Allyn & Bacon.

Johnson, D.W. and Johnson, R. (1992) *Positive Interdependence: The Heart of Cooperative Learning*. Edina, MI: Interaction Book Company.

Jones, A.V. (1987) Working together: the development of an integration programme in a primary school, *Cambridge Journal of Education*, 17(3): 175–8.

Jordan, A. (1994) *Skills in Collaborative Classroom Consultation*. London: Routledge.

Kahn, R.L., Wolfe, D., Quinn, R., Snoek, J. and Rosenthal, R. (1964) *Organizational Stress: Studies in Role Conflict and Ambiguity*. New York: Wiley.

Katzenbach, J. and Smith, D. (1993) *The Wisdom of Teams*. Cambridge, MA: Harvard Business School Press.

Kawahito, K. and Kiyoshi, Y. (1990) Labour relations in the Japanese automobile and steel industries, *Journal of Labour Research*, 11(3): 231.

Kennedy, K.T. and Duthie, J.H. (1975) *Auxiliaries in the Classroom: A Feasibility Study in Scottish Primary Schools*. HMSO: Edinburgh.

Kersell, J. (1990) Team management and development in Montserrat and Anguila, *Public Administration and Development*, 10: 81–91.

Kolvin, I., Garside, R.F., Nichol, A.R., Macmillan, A., Wolstenholme, F. and Leitch, I.M. (1981) *Help Starts Here: The Maladjusted Child in the Ordinary School*. London: Tavistock.

Kounin, J. (1970) *Discipline and Group Management in Classrooms*. New York: Holt, Rinehart & Winston.

Lacey, P. (1999) *On a Wing and a Prayer: Inclusion and Children with Severe Learning Difficulties*. London: Mencap.

Lacey, P. (2001) *Support Partnerships: Collaboration in Action*. London: David Fulton.

Le Laurin, K. and Risley, T.R. (1972) The organisation of day care environments: zone v man to man staff assignments, *Journal of Applied Behaviour Analysis*, 5(3): 225–32.

Lee, B. and Mawson, C. (1998) *Survey of Classroom Assistants*. Slough: NFER and UNISON.

Leigh, A. (1996) No pain, no gain: why teamwork is worth it, *People Management*, 2(10): 47–9.

Leyden, G. (1996) 'Cheap labour' or neglected resource? The role of the peer group and efficient, effective support for children with special needs, *Educational Psychology in Practice*, 11(4): 49–55.

Lindelow, J. and Bentley, S. (1989) Team management, in S.C. Smith and P.K. Piele (eds) *School Leadership Handbook for Excellence*, 2nd edn, pp. 135–51.

Linder, T. (1990) *Transdisciplinary Play-based Assessment*. Baltimore, MD: Paul Brookes.

Lorenz, S. (1998) *Effective In-Class Support: The Management of Support Staff in Mainstream and Special Schools*. London: David Fulton.

Losen, S. and Losen, J. (1994) Action research for professional practice: a position paper on educational action research, Paper presented at the annual conference of BERA, September.

Lowe, J. (1991) Teambuilding via outdoor training: experiences from a UK automotive plant, *Human Resource Management Journal*, 2(1): 42–59.

Loxley, A., Bhatti, G. and Swann, W. (1997) Moving beyond the fringe: school-based training for classroom assistants, in S. Shah (ed.) *Proceedings of the Inaugural Conference of the Centre for Equality Issues in Education*. Watford: University of Hertfordshire.

Lucas, D. and Thomas, G. (2000) Organising classrooms to promote learning for all children: two pieces of action research, in S. Clipson-Boyles (ed.) *Putting Research into Practice in Primary Teaching and Learning.* London: David Fulton.

Magjuka, R. and Baldwin, T. (1991) Team-based employee involvement programs: effect of design and administration, *Personnel Psychology*, 44: 793–812.

Marks, S.U., Schrader, C. and Levine, M. (1999) Paraeducator experiences in inclusive settings: helping, hovering, or holding their own? *Exceptional Children*, 65: 315–28.

Maslow, A. (1962) *Towards a Psychology of Being.* Princeton, NJ: Van Nostrand.

Matsui, M., Kakuyama, T. and Onglateo, M. (1987) Effects of goals and feedback on performance in groups, *Journal of Applied Psychology*, 72(3): 416–25.

McBrien, J. and Weightman, J. (1980) The effects of room management procedures on the engagement of profoundly retarded children, *British Journal of Mental Subnormality*, 26(1): 38–46.

Messick, D. and Brewer, M. (1983) Solving social dilemmas: a review, in L. Wheeler and P. Shaver (eds) *Review of Personality and Social Psychology*, 4: 11–44.

Miskin, V. and Gmelch, W. (1985) Quality leadership for quality teams, *Training and Development Journal*, 39(5): 122–9.

Mitchell, T. and Silver, W. (1990) Individual and group goals when workers are interdependent: effects on task strategies and performance, *Journal of Applied Psychology*, 75(2): 185–93.

Mohrman, S. and Ledford, G.R. (1985) The design and use of effective employee participation groups: implications for human resource managers. *Human Resource Management*, 24: 413–28.

Morgan, C. and Murgatroyd, S. (1994) *Total Quality Management in the Public Sector.* Buckingham: Open University Press.

Moyles, J. and Suschitzky, W. (1997) *Jills of all Trades? Classroom Assistants in KS1 Classes.* London: ATL Publications.

NACCCE (National Advisory Committee on Creative and Cultural Education) (1999) *All Our Futures: Creativity, Culture and Education.* Sudbury: DfEE.

Newton, C., Taylor, G. and Wilson, D. (1996) Circles of friends: an inclusive approach to meeting emotional and behavioural needs, *Educational Psychology in Practice*, 11(4): 41–8.

Ofsted (Office for Standards in Education) (1995) *Class Size and the Quality of Eduction.* London: Ofsted.

Ofsted (Office for Standards in Education) (2002) *Teaching Assistants in Primary Schools: An Evaluation by Ofsted 2001–2002.* London: Ofsted.

Parker-Rees, R. (1999) Time to relax a little: making time for the interplay of minds in education, *Education*, 28(1): 29–35.

Penn, H. and McQuail, S. (1997) *Childcare as a Gendered Occupation.* London: DfEE.

Peters, T. and Waterman, R. (1982) *In Search of Excellence.* New York: Harper & Rowe.

Pfluger, L.W. and Zola, J.M. (1974) A room planned by children, in G.J. Coates (ed.) *Alternative Learning Environments.* Stroudsburg, PA: Dowden, Hutchinson & Ross.

Phares, E.J. (1957) Expectancy changes in skill and chance situations, *Journal of Abnormal and Social Psychology*, 54: 339–42.

Porterfield, J., Blunden, R. and Blewitt, E. (1977) *Improving Environments for Profoundly Handicapped Adults: Establishing Staff Routines for High Client Engagement.* Cardiff: Mental Handicap in Wales Applied Research Unit, University of South Wales, Cardiff.

Pugach, M.C. and Johnson, L.J. (1990) Meeting diverse needs through professional peer collaboration, in W. Stainback and S. Stainback (eds) *Support Networks for Inclusive Schooling: Interdependent Integrated Education.* Baltimore, MD: Paul H. Brookes.

Rainbird, H. (1994) The changing role of the training function: a test for the integration of human resources and business strategies, *Human Resource Management Journal*, 5(1): 72–90.

Rainforth, B. *et al.* (1992) *Collaborative Teams for Students with Severe Disabilities.* Baltimore, MD: Paul Brookes.

Randle, K. and Brady, N. (1997) Further education and the new managerialism, *Journal of Further and Higher Education*, 21(2): 229–39.

Roberts, B. and Dyson, A. (2002) *Final Evaluation Report of the Learning Support Assistants Project.* Newcastle upon Tyne: Special Needs Research Centre, School of Education, Communication and Language Skills, University of Newcastle upon Tyne.

Rogers, C.R. (1951) *Client-centred Therapy.* Boston, MA: Houghton Mifflin.

Rose, R. (2000) Using classroom support in a primary school: a single school case study, *British Journal of Special Education*, 27: 191–6.

Rottier, J. (1996) Group work in education, *Education Digest*, 62(2): 19–23.

Salisbury, C., Gallucci, C., Palombaro, M.M. and Peck, C.A. (1995) Strategies that promote social relations among elementary students with and without severe disabilities in inclusive schools, *Exceptional Children*, 62(2): 125–37.

Saur, R.E., Popp, M.J. and Isaacs, M. (1984) Action zone theory and the hearing impaired student in the mainstreamed classroom, *Journal of Classroom Interaction*, 19(2): 21–5.

Scarp, L. (1982) For effective school leadership, keep your management team on the right track, *Executive Educator*, 4: 12–50.

Schön, D.A. (1987) Educating the reflective practitioner. Presentation to the Annual Meeting of the American Educational Research Association, Washington DC. Available at http://educ.queensu.ca/~ar/schon87.htm

Schön, D.A. (1991) *The Reflective Practitioner: How Professionals Think in Action*. Aldershot: Avebury.

Senge, P. (1990) *The Fifth Discipline*. New York: Doubleday.

Shaw, M. (1981) *Group Dynamics: The Psychology of Small Group Behaviour*. New York: McGraw-Hill.

Shea, G. and Guzzo, R. (1987) Group effectiveness: what really matters, *Sloan Management Review*, 3: 25–31.

Shonk, J. (1992) *Team-based Organisations: Developing a Successful Team Environment*. Homewood: Business One Irwin.

Smith, K., Kenner, C. and Barton-Hide, D. (1999) *Research Project: Career Ladder for Classroom Assistants*. Southampton: University of Southampton/Hampshire County Council.

Snell, M.E. and Janney, R. (2000) *Collaborative Teaming*. Baltimore, MD: Paul Brookes Publishing.

Strain, P.S. and Kerr, M.M. (1981) *Mainstreaming of Children in Schools: Research and Programmatic Issues*. London: Academic Press.

Sundstrom, E., De Muse, K. and Futrell, D. (1990) Work teams: applications and effectiveness. *American Psychologist*, 45: 120–33.

Swann, W. (1988) Learning difficulties or curricular reform: integration or differentiation? in G. Thomas and A. Feiler (eds) *Planning for Special Needs: A Whole School Approach*. Oxford: Basil Blackwell.

Tann, S. (1988) Grouping and the integrated classroom, in G. Thomas and A. Feiler (eds) *Planning for Special Needs*. Oxford: Blackwell.

Thomas, G. (1985) Room management in mainstream education, *Educational Research*, 27(3): 186–93.

Thomas, G. (1987) Extra people in the primary classroom, *Educational Research*, 29(3): 173–82.

Thomas, G. (1991) Defining role in the new classroom teams, *Educational Research*, 33(3): 186–99.

Thomas, G. (1992) *Effective Classroom Teamwork: Support or Intrusion?* London: Routledge.

Thomas, G., Walker, D. and Webb, J. (1998) *The Making of the Inclusive School*. London: Routledge.

Tizard, J., Schofield, W.N. and Hewison, J. (1982) Collaboration between teachers and parents in assisting children's reading, *British Journal of Educational Psychology*, 52: 1–15.

Tjosvold, D. (1991) *Team Organisation: An Enduring Competitive Advantage*. Chichester: John Wiley.

TTA (Teacher Training Agency) (2003) *Professional Standards for Higher Level Teaching Assistants*. London: TTA.

Udvari-Solner, A. and Thousand, J. (1995) Effective organisational, instructional and curricular practices in inclusive schools and classrooms, in C. Clarke, A. Dyson and A. Millward (eds) *Towards Inclusive Schools?* London: Fulton.

Vincett, K. (2001) How can we deploy LSAs to develop independence in pupils? Unpublished research paper, Essex County Council.

Vygotsky, L.S. (1978) *Mind and Society: The Development of Higher Mental Processes.* Cambridge, MA: Harvard University Press.

Wallen, R. (1963) Three types of executive personality, *Dun's Review*, December.

Watkinson, A. (1998) Supporting learning and assisting teaching: the teacher – the assistant – the learner, *Topic*, 19.

Watkinson, A. (1999) The use and deployment of teaching assistants in Essex primary schools in the summer of 1998, *Education Research Digest*, 3:99 (Essex County Council).

Weinstein, C.S. (1979) The physical environment of the school: a review of the research, *Review of Educational Research*, 49(4): 577–610.

Welch, A.R. (1998) The cult of efficiency in education: comparative reflections on the reality and the rhetoric, *Comparative Education*, 34(1): 157–75.

Welch, M., Richards, G., Okada, T., Richards, J. and Prescott, S. (1995) A consultation and paraprofessional pull-in system of service delivery: a report on student outcomes and teacher satisfaction, *Remedial and Special Education*, 16: 16–28.

West, M.A. (2000) Creativity and innovation at work, *The Psychologist*, 13: 460–4.

West-Burnham, J. (1991) Human resource management in schools, in B. Davies *et al.* (eds) *Education for the 1990s.* Harlow: Longman.

Whalley, M. (1992) Working as a team, in G. Pugh, (ed.) *Contemporary Issues in the Early Years.* London: Paul Chapman.

Wheldall, K. (1988) The forgotten A in behaviour analysis: the importance of ecological variables in classroom management with particular reference to seating arrangements, in G. Thomas and A. Feiler (eds) *Planning for Special Needs: A Whole School Approach.* Oxford: Basil Blackwell.

Wheldall, K., Morriss, M., Vaughan, P. and Ng, Y.Y. (1981) Rows v. tables: an example of the use of behavioral ecology in two classes of eleven-year-old children, *Educational Psychology*, 1(2): 171–84.

Wood, J. (1994) Shared or joint training? in J. Harris and J. Corbett (eds) *Training and Professional Development.* Kidderminster: BILD.

Woods, P. (1995) *Creative Teachers in Primary Schools.* Buckingham: Open University Press.

Index